ISLAM

IN

BRITAIN

PAST, PRESENT AND THE FUTURE

Mohammad S. Raza

V·O·L·C·A·N·O
PRESS LTD

First published in paperback 1991
Volcano Press Ltd.,
P.O. Box 139,
Leicester LE2 2YH

British Library Cataloguing in Publication Data
Raza, Mohammad, Shahid
  Islam in Britain: past present and the future
  1. Great Britain. Muslims
  I. Title
  305.6971041

ISBN 1 870127 35 8

Printed and bound in England by
Bassett Enterprises Ltd.,
Dunton Bassett,
Leicestershire.

Contents

Introduction

The idea of writing this study had been in my mind for many years. Recent events in Britain lent it urgency. One of which was the Rushdie affair and the other – even more recent – the Gulf crisis. Both of these events focused much negative attention on the Muslim community in Britain. A great deal of misinformation and disinformation was unwittingly or, in some instances, deliberately spread by various groups in British society, so that I thought the time had come to challenge such assumptions and set the record straight. I do not, however, claim to have written the last word on this vast subject. But I hope that this study will initiate other works on the same subject.

At the beginning of the project a number of questions needed to be addressed. First, I had to decide which Muslim community needed to be investigated. I selected those migrants who had come from the Indo-Pakistan sub-continent as they constitute the majority of Muslims in Britain. Furthermore, I was familiar with their culture and customs as all my theological training had been in the religious institutions of Indo-Pakistan.

The second question was: what aspects of this complex community needed to be covered? Obviously, in a short study one could not cover all aspects. I selected only those which are of major concern to the community itself. As can be seen by any Imam who deals with people at the grassroot level, many of their concerns could be identified by me in this study. I found that there are as many opinions as there are community leaders. In fact, one could enlarge each chapter into a separate book. What I have done is to pull together the major trends of opinion and developed each topic in sufficient depth. My objective being to provide the reader with little or no knowledge with a cognitive map reflecting a general picture of the Muslim community in Britain at the present time.

Third, the study of the Muslim community can be approached from many different perspectives, such as ethnicity or class, etc. I chose the variable of Islam which directly or indirectly exerts an influence on the lives of the majority of Muslims in Britain. My investigations focused on the formations which emerged in the community's interaction with Islam on one hand, and with the secular society on the other. The foremost question in my mind was how the Muslim community endeavours to live an Islamic life in a secular society? My purpose was to portray the realities that exist and not what ought to be. However the Muslim community must face up to the truth, no matter how unpalatable.

Finally, it is not enough to highlight the social conditions which prevail in the Muslim community or to blame the West for its social problems. It is necessary to acknowledge the contradictions that exist within the Muslim community itself. The study therefore takes a critical approach that is both constructive and foresighted.

It could be argued that it is easy to criticise but what are the solutions? Wherever possible, some prescriptions have been given bearing in mind the internal and external factors affecting the community. One cannot, however, propose solutions without reference to the context in the community in which one is resident, or without looking at the long-term prospects in such a context. In other words, the Muslim community needs to have a vision of its future role in Western societies. Every generation has to leave something substantive for the next. Future generations should not be left groping in the dark in the secular society.

The materials consulted in writing this study have been helpful. All the sources have been acknowledged. The omissions, if any, have not been deliberate. Above all, I am indebted to my friend, Asaf Hussain, from the Muslim Community Studies Institute. He read the manuscript, discussed a number of points and allowed me permission to use some of the first-hand data collected by MCSI.

Mohammad S. Raza   February 1991
Leicester

Chapter 1 *The Cultural Fabric*

Culture is a powerful force in society. The term, 'in its broadest definition, refers to that part of the total repertoire of human action (and its products), which is socially as opposed to genetically transmitted'.[1] Every generation learns the culture of the past generation and can act in a meaningful manner which is understood in that society. In Britain, British culture characterized its society and differentiated itself from the cultures of other countries like France and Germany. British society may also have a number of variations on the basis of the national-ethnic subcultures of the English, Welsh, Scottish and Irish peoples. Similarly the large immigrant minorities will be reflecting their own cultures and customs, which will be different from the mainstream British culture. It is essential to focus on the cultural fabric of any minority before examining other aspects of it.

The cultural fabric of the Muslim community reveals an intricate web. The influences of some factors have posed as obstacles to a singular cultural manifestation. Most of these factors have not originated in the British context but from different sources of their country of origin. The national cultures of Pakistanis, Iranians, Arabs, Turks, Malaysians, Africans, etc. are all different from each other just as their language, clothes, food, etc are. National cultural traits, norms, and customs therefore have to be carefully distinguished from Islamic culture. For example, the fact all Muslim males are circumcised is Islamic but female circumcision is un-Islamic. The fact that females are subjected to this horrendous practice in some parts of Sudan has its origins in the Pharaonic and not the Islamic sanction. Similarly marriage between Muslims irrespective of caste, colour or nationaility is Islamic but marriages exclusively

1

within a *Biraderi* (extra-familial kinship ties) system is cultural and non-Islamic. Similarly greetings and invocations like *'Assalam Alaykum'* ('peace be upon you'), *'Alhamdulillah'* ('All praise be to Allah') and *'Insha Allah'* ('Allah willing') are part of Islamic culture and not exclusive to Pakistani, Arab, Iranian and Turkish cultures. Since these cultures follow Islam, these greetings are universal among them. However, within a Muslim community, national/ ethnic cultural characteristics may tend to dominate more than Islam. These are reflections of the national/ethnic cultures of the country of origin of Muslims. The national and ethnic factor for example strongly dominates Pakistani culture. Since the focus of this study is mainly on Asian Muslim minorities originating from Indo-Pakistan, the cultural variations of this largest group will be explained.

This ethnic factor divides the Pakistanis in Britain. Since migration has not been in substantial numbers from all provinces but mainly from the Punjab and Mirpur, the division is mainly between these two and manifests itself in ethnic organization. But national and ethnic identities have meant that each ethnic group, such as the Bangladeshis, Gujaratis, Punjabis and Mirpuris, has retained control over its own mosques and religious organizations. Nationalism and ethnicity have therefore kept the influence of Islam at bay. Ethnicity has its own social control systems in terms of *Biraderi,* caste and tribal affiliations.[2]

Within an ethnic group even sharper distinctions can exist within ethnic communities on the bases of kinship, which as mentioned above is known as *Biraderis*. Literally *Biraderi* means brotherhood and 'includes all the men who can trace their relationship to a common ancestor, no matter how remote...The decent group *Biraderi* includes all those who claim and can trace links of a common paternal line. As Pakistani society is a patrilineal all the inheritance is through the male line and so is the *Biraderi'*.[3] The *Biraderi* system has a patriarchal base, which is the natural ancient order of most societies. But the ranking system which developed amongMuslims of the Indian subcontinent is definitely influenced by the Hindu caste system. Most Muslims were Hindu converts and it was easy for the *Zat* system to penetrate. Blunt distinguishes the differences between *Zat* (caste) and *Biraderis* in his study by observing that 'the *Zat* is the caste as a whole; the *Biraderi* is the group of caste brethren who live in particular neighbourhoods and act together for caste purposes. The *Biraderi* quantitatively considered is a mere fraction of the *Zat* qualitatively considered, it is the *Zat* in action'.[4] The *Zat* system ranks various groups in a hierarchical manner and one researcher on Pakistanis in Britain correctly observes that 'Muslims in the Indian subcontinent are very conscious of ranks despite the egalitarianism implicit in Islam'.[5] Such *Zat* systems as Arians, Rajas and Rajputs are widespread among Pakistanis and reflect the fact that Islamic egalitarianism has not been firmly rooted. If it had, then *Zat* consciousness would be extremely weak, which is not the case.

The *Biraderi* system provides a security network. Its cultural code of operation is *Vartan Bhanji* (exchange of gifts) which 'involves exchange of sweets, fruits, food, money and yards of cloth; extending beyond material things, it includes the exchange of services, favours, like treatment, entertainment and participation in ceremonial events. In its operation, this mechanism of exchange involves a whole range of relationships among the *Biraderi* and other groups who make up the Punjabi society. It is of vital importance to people as a means of achieving *Izzat* (prestige)'.[6] Its influence operates in welfare, political and economic areas in the life of the ethnic community. The *Biraderi* system has no links with Islam. Similarly among the Pathans, the Code of *Pakhtunwali* with its features of *tora* (courage), *badal* (revenge), *melmastia* (hospitality), etc. is considered by tribal Pathans to be legitimised by Islam.[7]

Nationalism is another very important factor in creating divisions among the Muslims in general. For example, after the creation of Pakistan, ethnic and national identities emerged emphasizing its culture, history and languages. These began to manifest themselves more strongly than religion. The Pathans of North West Frontier Province, Baluchis from Baluchistan, Sindhis from Sind, Punjabis from Punjab, all manifested the strong predominant nature of ethnic nationalists. So strong is the ethnic factor in Pakistan that it led to the emergence of ethnic nationalism. According to Dr. Zaki Badawi, 'Muslims differ slightly in their acts of worship and personal ethical values but they differ widely in their politics. Attempts to inject Muslim political behaviour with the unifying spirit of Islam have failed...Politicians have often manipulated their faith rather than sought guidance from it. Ambitious warriors employed scholars to legitimise their conquests. Ardent revolutionaries scoured the Holy Qu'ran or the Traditions of the Prophet to justify their actions and policies. The failure of Muslims to derive from their faith a bond of political unity is manifested by the break up of Pakistan into Bangladesh and Pakistan. The original Pakistan of 1947 was the very country which came into existence to be a home for all Muslims'.[8] The creation of Bangladesh however has not abated the ethnic problem of Pakistan. It has given rise to the 'four nationalities' questions emanating from the four provinces of Pakistan: Baluchistan, Punjab, Sind and North West Frontier Province. More recently another call has also joined the four nationalities. This has come from the Urdu speaking *Muhajirs* who migrated from India to Pakistan in 1947. They want to be recognized as the fifth nationality on the basis of their language, Urdu. This is one of the demands of their political group in Karachi (Pakistan), the *Muhajir Quami Mahaz* Movement.

In all of this 'nationalities' question, Islam has played a

very small role, although Pakistani culture follows a number of Islamic social festivals which have been integrated into the ethnic-national and social customs. These are *Ashurah* (commemoration of the martyrdom of Imam Hussain, grandson of the Prophet Muhammad, on the 10th day of the month of Muharram in the Islamic calendar); *Milad un Nabi* (birthday of the Prophet on the 12th day of the month of Rabi al-Awal of the Islamic calendar); *Laylat al-Qadr* (observed on the 27th night of the fasting of the Islamic month of Ramadan); *Idd ul Fitr* (celebration after the fasting is over on the first day of the Islamic month of Shawwal); and *Idd ul-Adha* (celebration of the sacrifice made by the Prophet Ibrahim) on the 10th day of the Islamic month of Dhulhijjah). These are some of the major celebrations.[9] Ethnicity and religion are inter-related and the mechanism operates as a means of social control within each ethnic group. From the ethnic side it may have cultural customs and *Biraderi* and *Zat* traditions while Islam is often used to legitimize most of them.

Conclusion
In general, the ethnic cultural systems are all rooted in the patriarchal order. They existed before the advent of Islam. The latter was used to legitimize this patriarchal order. The Punjabi ethnic cultural interpretation of Islam will legitimize the *Biraderi* system as much as the Pathan cultural ethnics will legitimize their *Pakhtunwali*. Because of this utilization of Islam — the legitimizing link — any threat to national cultural values is often confused as a threat to Islam. It not only shows an ignorance but a limited understanding of Islam and a lack of Islamic culture. Ideally every Muslim society would like to think that it enjoys 'Islamic' culture and the Muslim community in Britain and Indo-Pakistan considers that to be the case. But the veneer of Islamic culture is spread thinly.

In Britain social class stratification takes place on the basis of its relationship to occupation. The Registrar General's classification dividing classes into professional, intermediate, skilled non-manual, skilled manual, partly skilled and unskilled categories reflects it.[1] Members of British society irrespective of whether they are Muslim or non-Muslims can all be found in this six-tiered social class structure. But Asians have not been assimilated into the British class structure because racism creates the divide that separates them. So within the working classes in the last three categories of the Registrar General's classification the 'white' working class clubs or residential areas will not accept the coloureds even though they may be living side by side in terraced housing estates. Similarly, in the upper class residential areas, there may not be the blatant racist hostility manifested in the housing estates, but snobbery may not allow any mingling of neighbours.

But social class among Asians is not guided by occupation. Among Asians social class is determined by income and not occupation. Occupations are selected to earn higher wages. Education and other skills are acquired in order to earn higher incomes and not to be assimilated into the English middle or upper classes. As stated earlier, not only does racism forbid such assimilation but even the historical experiences of each class are different. Children of English parents may become assimilated into the English middle classes on the basis of their occupations because the Industrial Revolution broke rigid class barriers and children struggled to improve the class of their parents. But a Muslim illiterate peasant who migrated to Britain never ever was part of the class struggle in Britain or was able to identify with it.

His children may have the same occupation but they do not have the same history or class conciousnes; nor can they be assimilated into the middle or working classes. They may not fulfil and fit the Registrar General's categories but they do have the class conciousness of the British people.

What exists is a status elite among the Muslim Asian community due to the subjective status perception by members of the community. Similar status groups are also found among the black middle classes in the USA. [2] The Muslims in Britain are upwardly mobile but not many are progressing up the social ladder in terms of the Registrar General's class stratification.[3]

Under the broad label of status-elites there are a number of sub-status groups, whose status is determined by one or more factors. One such subjective factor is wealth. The business elites may be totally illiterate but have made it though wealth. They may own paltial houses and Rolls-Royces, send their children to private schools, etc. They may not be part of the English upper classes in similar positions but are perceived by the Muslim community as a status-elite.

In another category, on the same continuum, the emphasis is placed on education. Those Muslims who have become doctors, dentists, chartered accountants, barristers and solicitors, educationalists, etc. are the professional status-elites. They have little in common with the business elites, whose lack of education creates a social distance which keeps them separate. One may boast of his wealth, the other of his education. The third category, in the same continuum, contains the traditional status-elites who may derive their status linkage from neither wealth nor education but a familial pedigree relating them to the Prophet's family and denoted by the prefix 'Syed' attached to their names. Some may come from a family of religious elites and may be referred to as 'Pirs' (spiritual guide). In the last category are the positional elites. They may have neither wealth, education nor pedigree but are holding some important positions within the British context. They may have gained these through, for example, being Justices of the Peace or they may have worked their way upwards and may be occupying some positions in the civil service (police, customs, etc.) semi-government organizations (Commission for Racial Equality), local government (councillors), etc. Since they are in a position of rendering a service they rank high in the eyes of the recipients.

In this immigrant context, income tends not only to provide security and fulfilment of migration objectives but also to fulfil the status requirement in the country of origin. Muslim migrants by building themselves a *Pakka* house (of kiln-baked bricks and mortar), by having lands with tube-wells and tractors, etc. in their country of origin may change their status from landless labourers and become persons of substance.[4] Most of the Muslims who dream of going back to their country of origin one day or who have dependents to support have done this. Others cannot do this even if they wanted to, such as the Asian Muslims from East Africa for they were driven out by Africans like Idi Amin of Uganda.

Whatever the case may be, the income and education factors in the British context may lead Asian Muslims into Westernized lifestyles and Western value systems. The income factor gives the buying power of lifestyles with the attendant trappings of the indigenous class symbols. Since they cannot be assimilated into the indigenous class system they can ape it. Similarly the education factor can also brainwash the individual into the indigenous class customs of British culture. The value system of Asian Muslims may have become secular and rooted in the secular ideologies of Britain.

Asian Muslims may drink, go to discos, have pre-marital

and extramarital relations and some even eat pork. By becoming Westernized they may ape Western class customs and mannerisms but cannot assimilate with ease as they are not accepted. On the other hand, there are a number of Muslims who belong to the various status-elites and who are Islamically oriented. They may try to legitimize their actions and attitudes through Islam. The most popular form is to donate money to the mosque or for mosque building. Some rich Muslims may even pay for the building of the mosques. Others may go for *Hajj* and think that by doing this they have done their duty to Islam. Another may even legitimize their drinking by saying: 'I don't serve alcohol in my home. But if I am called upon to toast the Queen in champagne, I don't hesitate. What it says in the Koran is don't drink and pray, not don't drink at all'.[5] There are others who consider themselves British, sell wine and whisky and consider it risky to invest in Pakistan. They are married to English women and reside in spacious houses.[6]

These are just two examples, but there are a number of Muslim millionaires in Britain who consider that God has bestowed special favours on them and they therefore owe some duties to Him. But this warped understanding of Islam only shows their ignorance of Islam, while in the long run they are going to be the losers. They have clung to their wealth as their only security. The result has been, as one Muslim commented about other rich Muslims, that 'virtually the only thing about them now which is Muslim is their name'.[7] The pursuit of money is their only goal in life and how it is earned does not concern them. In a *Khutba* (sermon) given in the London Islamic Cultural Centre, Shaikh Gamal Manna'a stated: 'It is horrifying to hear that some Muslims deal in liquor and pork. It would certainly be preferable to die from starvation in their own countries than grow wealthy or even comfortable on the proceeds of what is forbidden...It is a pity that people live un-Islamically in this country and acquire wealth with no worries at all about their own future or their children's.[8] The Muslim community is so sucked into the status trap that its vision of their future seems blurred.

Conclusion

It is sufficient to note here that the class system has divided the Muslim community. The poor Muslims have more faith in Islam than the status-elites. Few Muslims from the latter take their religion seriously. They may not be anti-Islamic but apart from rendering lip-service to Islam, they are more seriously engaged in accumulating money to be able to afford the status symbols and indulge in conspicuous consumption. In Islam wealth is a means towards achieving Islamic objectives. Where such wealth leads to personal status considerations, the Islamic commitment is not total but partial. When it becomes partial it only breeds a hypocritical attitude towards Islam.

One of the reasons which will be examined later in Chapter 5 as to why Muslims are travelling with the begging bowl to the Middle East for funds is because in Britain the spirit of giving donations is lagging. It is not a general fact that Muslims are not donating money. Some money is being donated but the motives are suspect. Sometimes it is to make a name for oneself in the community: in other cases it is to feel exonerated from a religious duty and think one has discharged one's duty. The motive to give money has to be for the sake of God and for the good of the community. The spirit of belonging to the community is lacking due to national/ethnic/class and status factors.

Chapter 3   *Sectarian Contexts*

Just as the Muslim community is divided by class stratification and ethnic boundaries, it is also divided by sectarianism. Before analysing sectarianism a discussion of the major sectarian divisions of the Muslim community in Britain would be in order.

The Barelvis
The majority of the Muslims in Britain belong to the Berelvi school of thought. In every city there are Berelvi mosques and Imams. Apart from the Imams there are also a number of Pirs (spiritual guides) who are related to the various Sufi orders in Indo-Pakistan. These men wield a lot of influence on the Imams belonging to their orders and in their own way render service to their communities.

Conflict with the Berelvis in Britain is usually on the very high sacred status which they give to the Prophet Muhammad. It is not surprising that they have also been at the forefront of the anti-Rushdie campaign in Britain due to the insult cast on the Prophet's life by Salman Rushdie's The Satanic Verses.

HISTORICAL ROOTS
The Barelvis are Sunni Muslims and generally follow the interpretaions of Islam of Maulana Ahmad Raza Khan (1856–1921) of Bareilly in India. Maulana Raza Khan was a renowned Hanifi scholar of *Ahl-i-Sunnat wa Jamaat,* which is another name by which Barelvis are known. The *Ahl-i-Sunnat* are followers of the Prophetic traditions and the Prophet's companions.

The Barelvi movement was a radical movement which did not accept the views of the *Deoband Ulama,* the *Ahl-e-*

Hadith and some others. All of these movements were influenced by the doctrines of an Arabian reformer, Muhammad ibn Al- Wahhab, whose followers were often known as *Wahhabis*. In his reforming zeal Abd al-Wahhab destroyed the graves of the companions and family of the Prophet Muhammad, claiming that grave worship had entered Islam. His influence began to penetrate India, and all the Islamic groups under Wahhabi influence stopped their followers from paying respects to the Islamic holy figures in Indo-Pakistan history. They also regarded the Prophet as an ordinary man and denied that he had any *Ilm-i-Ghaib* (knowledge of the unknown). Maulana Raza Khan's movement opposed all these movements through the *Fatwas* (religious edicts) which he issued and which had the approval of many of his contemporaries from Hejaz (now Saudi Arabia), Syria, Egypt and India.

The main thrust of the Barelvi movement was their overwhelming love of the Prophet Muhammad and the Barelvis defended his honour wherever it was under attack. When the Deobandis claimed that the Prophet could not have *Ilm-i-Ghaib* because he was only a man. Maulana Imam Raza Khan attacked them for distorting the doctrine of the finality of the Prophet Muhammad. Imam Raza Khan wrote many books on the various aspects of the life of the Prophet and *Fiqh* (jurisprudence). He also composed a long poem in his honour.[1] He also believed in the Sufi doctrine of *Nur-e-Muhammadi* (the light of Muhammad) 'which was derived from God's own light and had existed...from the beginning of creation. It was omnipresent; it meant that the Prophet though human was also more than human. He had, moreover, unique knowledge of the unknown *(Ilm-i-Ghaib)* and could be called upon to intercede for man with God'.[2]

The *Ahl-i-Sunnat wa Jamaat* celebrated the birthday of the Prophet *(Idd-i-Milad un-Nabi)* with great pomp and show where religious songs *(Naats)* were sung, food served, and and the life of the Prophet eulogized. They also celebrated the commemoration of Shaykh Abdul Qadir Gilani, a great Sufi saint buried in Baghdad (Iraq), and other prominent Sufi saints. In all these matters the other sects under Wahhabi influence did not agree with the Barelvis.

The Barelvis, as stated above, regard the Prophetic status as divinely bestowed and as such higher than ordinary man. Consequently, the Prophet is regarded with very high veneration. Those who try to malign the character of the Prophet would be the first to offend the Barelvis.

The Deobandis

The Deobandis are a break-a-way group of Sunni Muslims. They follow strictly the Ulama of Deoband and their interpretation of Islam. They have their own mosques and live quiet lives. The Deobandis do not show the high veneration for the Prophet that the Barelvis do. Islam is a personal and not a social religion for them.

According to one observer, 'they will have no concern to establish an Islamic state, indeed, they are unlikely to be interested in the state except in so far as it prevents them from fulfilling their quite narrowly conceived objectives'.[3] In their behaviour the Deobandis are subservient to authority.

HISTORICAL ROOTS

This attitude of subservience is rooted in the historical tradition of the Deobandis. The threat posed by the British Raj could have had three kinds of response from the Muslims. Firstly, they could have challenged them to remove the colonizers. Secondly, they could have compromised with them. Thirdly, they could have withdrawn into their own homes and left the field open to the colonizers. It is the third option which most of the Deobandis took and opened a

13

Madrassah (school) at Deoband, 90 miles from Delhi, the British colonial capital in India.

The teaching of the Deobandis was non-political and, as such, the British had no difficulty in introducing secular laws and an educational system relegating Islam to a position of insignificance. The teaching of the Deobandi seminary was so superficial that it did not produce any Muslims fit enough to challenge the secularist and modernist ideas penetrating into the country. In fact, for those Muslims who rose up to challenge the British colonial state, the Deobandis 'could not just support Pakistan which they envisaged as an Islamic state which would be ruled by secular Muslims. They saw a preferable future in a secular independent India where somewhat optimistically they hoped that some form of jurisprudential apartheid would be achieved'[4] with the Hindus. But when Pakistan was established they had no choice but to migrate to the new Muslim state. The Deobandi seminary, however, still functions in India.

The Tablighi Jamaat
The centre of the Tablighi Jamaat in Britain is Dewsbury. They are spread all over Britain through the mosques and are well organized. They are polite, courteous and well behaved, and can easily be spotted in the streets. They wear a cap, a beard, a long shirt which goes below the knees, and a pyjama or trousers which is shortened to be above the ankles. They might also wear a jacket and sneakers. They keep very much to themselves; according to Robinson, 'in Britain we would expect the Tabligh...to be the least involved in controversy of any kind'.[5]

HISTORICAL ROOTS
The founder of the Tablighi Jamaat in India was Maulana Muhammad Ilyas (1885–1944). A student of Deoband, he became disillusioned with the introverted Deobandis and

wanted to project Islam in an extroverted manner. His main thrust was to do missionary work and he formulated a six-point programme to achieve it, as follows: (1) the profession of faith; (2) ritually prescribed prayers; (3) knowledge and remembrance of God; (4) respect for all Muslims; (5)sincere intentions; and (6) the giving of time.[6] The Tablighis strictly adhere to these six points and travel in groups on *gasht* (tour) to bring other Muslims round to their way of thinking. They have been quite successful in this but like the Deobandis they are non-political.

The Ahl-e-Hadith

The Ahl-e-Hadith sect is not very large in Britain. One of its prominent centres is in Birmingham and, like the Deobandis it is a reformist movement. It did not put much faith in the various schools of jurisprudence such as the Hanifi and Malikis. It placed more responsibility on the individual by the 'use of jurisprudential techniques sanctioned by the Hadith (i.e. *qiyas* or argument by analogy and *ijma* or the consensus of the Ulama on a point of law)'. Like the Deobandis it was critical of the Sufis. It believed in an individualist approach. In the early 1970s the Ahl-e-Hadith organized themselves and they have branches in all the major cities in Britain as well as in a number of European ones. The membership has grown steadily and runs into many thousands'.[7] Two of their magazines are issued from Birmingham and are known as *The Straight Path* (in English) and *Sirat-e-Mustaqeem* (in Urdu).

HISTORICAL ROOTS

The Ahl-e-Hadith was again a reformist movement in search of a redefinition of the nature of Iman (faith). It was started at the end of the 19th century and by 1912 the All India Ahl-e-Hadith Conferences were held annually. The reformist movement took its cue from the two reformers, Shah Waliullah and Muhammad Ibn Abd al-Wahhab. Other 'pioneering members were Syed Nazeer Hussain of Delhi who founded the Madrasah Rahmania — one of the first Ahl-e-Hadith Madrassahs in India'.[8] Waliullah was trained in the Sufi traditions but was critical of many decadent traditions of Sufism on asceticism because of the influence of Wahhabism.

The Ahl-e-Hadith in their search for carving out a separate identity different from the Deobandis had a different style of beard and forms of prayers which led to their being banned from mosques by other sectarian groups in Indo-Pakistan. Such disputes were resolved by the State authorities.

The Pervaizi

Another reformist movement which has followers in Britain is the Pervaizi group. They are based in London and hold annual functions. They believe in the interpretation of the Qur'an, without the Hadith, as being authentic.

HISTORICAL ROOTS

Their historical roots can be traced to a splinter group from the Ahl-e-Hadith led by Abd Allah Chakralwi who named his movement as the Ahl-al-Quran movement. They emphasized the primacy of the Qur'an and nothing could equate with it. Two of its illustrious exponents were Inayat Allah al-Mashriqi (1888–1960) and Ghulam Ahmad Parvaiz (1903–1985). The Mashriqi's movement, which the *Khaksars* founded in 1931, was militant and believed that Muslims should aim for scientific advancement. To attain the vicegerency on earth (*Istikhlaf fil-Ard*) was the objective of the Muslims and they could better themselves by domination over nature.

The Modernists

Robinson identifies another group of Muslims which he labels as the Modernists. He further observes that they are found among the highly educated families of the second or third generation. However, 'their approach offers great opportunities for legal flexibility but to make public use of their understanding would be of little value as they do not have broad support in the community. For one thing, their elitism apart, their orientation has come under increasing attack as the Muslim revival has gathered way over the past thirty years; for another, their approach is more likely to succeed in those places where Muslims wield power as opposed to those where they are in a minority and feel threatened by another civilization'.[9] These observations are correct. The two men whom he identifies as important are Sayyad Ahmad Khan and Muhammad Iqbal (1877–1938), yet the two men cannot be labelled as 'modernists'. Sayyad Ahmad Khan was not a thinker of the calibre of Iqbal and his learning was not as extensive as the latter's. Sayyad Ahmad Khan arose as employee of the British, of whom he was an admirer, and they used him to set up educational institutions through which Western ideas could be transmitted.

The Revivalists

Muhammad Iqbal was a philosopher and attained his educational degrees from Western universities but his approach to Islam was not a compromising one like Sayyad Ahmad Khan's and instead challenged the West. His main medium of expressing his thoughts was poetry and he acknowledged that his intellect had been sharpened by Western learning as he had studied law and philosphy at London, Cambridge and Heidelberg, but his heart was enlightened by Muslim Sufis such as Jalaluddin Rumi (1209–1273) and others. He believed that only imbibing Western learning would 'shake men's convictions' and drive the 'bind of faith' away. Western civilization, he believed, would kill itself by its own dagger for, without faith, it had no future.

On the other hand, Iqbal was critical of the Muslims for

'just as the Brahmin has adorned his shelf with his idols, likewise) you too have placed the Qur'an on the shelf (as an adornment and nothing more)'.[10] Instead what Iqbal wanted is expressed in another poem:

> *I am revealing what is in my heart.*
> *This is not a book — but something mysteriously*
> *different.*
> *When life is saturated with it (the Quran)*
> *Life becomes different*
> *And when life becomes different, the world becomes*
> *different.*[11]

Iqbal also believed that:

> *The life that admits of non revolution amounts to*
> *death*
> *For, the life of the spirit of nations, consists in a*
> *struggle for revolution.*[12]

Iqbal believed that the Muslim should develop his self *(Khudi)* in three ways: (1) obedience to the law of God; (2) self-control of the self; and (3) taking the role of vicegerency on earth of God. Iqbal therefore advised the Muslims in *Javed Nameh:*

> *O Muslims, Remember, you cannot construct your*
> *life by imitating others.*
> *A living nation is capable of creating new worlds*
> *through its own thoughts and deeds.*
> *Therefore if you have the determination of real*
> *Muslims, then look into your self and delve deep into*
> *the Quran.*
> *You will discover that its verses hide hundreds of*
> *new worlds and its moments conceal thousands of*
> *new eras.*[13]

In order to solve the present problems only the application of a single point of the Qu'ran is sufficient:

> *But you can comprehend this point only if your*
> *breast contains an understanding heart.*
> *A Muslim is one of the signs of God and hence has*
> *the vitality to servive and progress in every age.*

This in a nutshell is Iqbal's inspiring understanding of Islam and within this general framework he sought to create an ideal Islamic man, the *Mard-e-Momin.* Anyone aspiring to become the *Mard-e-Momin* 'was to reach the stage of *Maqam-e-Kibriya* — the ultimate reality of reaching God, the role of vicegerency of God on earth. When the *Mard-e-Momin* had achieved these then the religious ideal of man is not self-negation, but self-affirmation, and he attains this ideal by becoming more and more individual, more and more unique'.[14]

Iqbal proposed the creation of a separate homeland for Muslims at the All India Muslim League's meeting in 1930 which ultimately led to the creation of Pakistan in 1947. In Britain he has a following both among the old and young. Some organizations such as the Iqbal Academy produced studies of Iqbal while Cambridge University has a post for an Iqbal Fellow (Chair in Pakistan Studies). There is no doubt that Iqbal's influence on other Muslim revolutionary thinkers like Ali Shariati from Iran has been profound. As a revivalist, he inspires Muslims and is considered the national philosopher of Pakistan.

The Jamaat-i-Islami
The followers of this political party are not many in Britain as compared to other sects. The Jamaat-i-Islami operate through various institutions of publishing books, new magazines, youth movements and mission organizations. All these are funded by Saudi Arabia for they follow the Wahhabi doctrines. They have not been able to influence the youth by their non-revolutionary thinking for they believe in maintaining the status quo of the Saudi Arabian royal family; while the Muslim youth influenced by the revolutionary Islam of other Muslim thinkers has lost faith in the monarchy.

HISTORICAL ROOTS
The Jamaat-i-Islami was founded by Maulana Abul Ala Mawdudi (1903–1979). Mawdudi started the political party

in the late 1920s and it opposed the creation of Pakistan on the basis that nationalism was alien to Islam. The Mawdudis have not converted Pakistan into an Islamic state, Islamized the military, or established grassroot influence with the masses in Pakistan who could vote them into power. But since the party is the recipient of large funds from Saudi Arabia, it operates as an elite party of the Pakistani bourgeoisie without possessing the capacity to address the needs of the masses in the country.

The Shi'ite Muslims

The Shi'ite Muslims are a minority in Britain. Apart from Shi'ites from the Indo-Pakistan subcontinent and other countries, some 25,000 Iranians are estimated to be in Britain.[15] Ever since the Islamic revolution took place in Iran, it has created Islamic reverberations in the Muslim world and direct confrontations have taken place with the Western forces such as the US and its satellites in Lebanon. The Shi'ites from Iran living in Britain have been under close watch since 1979. This became evident with *The Satanic Verses* when Ayatollah Khomeini issued his *Fatwa* against the life of the author, Salman Rushdie: some Iranian Shi'ites were immediately deported to Iran. In March 1989, some 17 Iranians were deported; in December 1989, two Iranians were again deported under the Prevention of Terrorism Act and in January 1990, nine Iranian students were deported.[16] The Shi'ites, due to their activist commitment to Islam, are taken seriously.

The Shi'ites are a well-knit community, and the influences of revolutionary Islam and its writers like Ayatollah Khomeini, Ali Shariati and Ayatollah Mohtahhari have exercised a considerable influence on the minds of the younger generation.

HISTORICAL ROOTS

The Shi'ite-Sunni dispute is the first and oldest sectarian

20

schism within early Islam. The Shi'ites believe that, after the death of the Prophet Muhammad, the first Caliph should have been Caliph Ali Ibn Talib, the Prophet's cousin and son-in-law who was married to his daughter. They wanted the Caliphate to pass on to the direct descendants of the Prophet and consider Ali as their first Imam. Instead Imam Ali became the fourth Caliph, and three others preceded him: Abu Bakr (632-634 AD), Umar Ibn al-Khattab (634-644 AD) and Uthman (644-656 AD). This dispute over leadership has lingered through history for the Imamate (descendants of the Prophet) became a threat to the Sunni Sultanate (monarchy) who labelled themselves as the Caliphs.

The Shi'ites follow their own school of Islamic jurisprudence *(fiqh)* given by the sixth Imam Jafar al-Sadiq (d. 765 AD) and known as the Jaffari *fiqh,* while the Sunnis follow the Sunni jurisprudents Ahmed Ibn Hanbal (d. 855), Abu Hanifa (d. 767), Muhammad al-Shafii (d. 820) and Malik ibn Anas (d. 795). The Shi'ite *fiqh* is recognized as a seperate *fiqh* by Sunni establishments such as Al Azhar.

Orientalist Islam
Orientalism is the Western view of Islam. It is a distorted Western perspective of Islam created by Western scholars. In all the institutions of Britain where Islamic studies is taught as a discipline and masters and doctoral degrees are awarded, Orientalist Islam is taught. Muslims attracted to belief in Orientalist Islam are secularized or Westernized.

HISTORICAL ROOTS
The Orientalist approach to Islam emanated from the West. As an intellectual discipline Orientalism developed to aid Western countries to consolidate their colonial hold on non-Western countries particularly in the Muslim world. Its objective was 'to deny and disprove the Prophet's status as

21

such and the Qur'an as revelation'.[17]

Consequently British Orientalist missionaries believed that as soon as the 'legend of Muhammad' crumbles and 'his character is seen in its true light' then the 'entire fabric must go' and then Christian preachers should 'save these people...for Christianity'.[18] Another British Orientalist missionary believed that 'Muhammad appears to have tried to mould Islam as the older religion' rather than Judaism. He speculated that had the Jews come to terms with Prophet Muhammad, Islam could have become 'a sect of Jewry'.[19] In order to discredit Islam as a 'way of life' it was considered to be an imitation of the religions of Judaism and Christianity. Furthermore, it follows that if Islam was a mongrelized form of Christianity or Judaism then like the latter Islam was separated from politics. Political Islam was then considered an aberration which had to be suppressed. This suited the colonialization objective of subjugating the colonized. Lastly, it was considered that since religion was separated from politics then, like in the West, secularization should exist, with religion becoming purely a spiritual and personal matter. Religion was replaced with secularization which 'involves the expansion of the polity at the expense of religion as major areas of social life (education, law, economy and so on) pass from religious regulation to the jurisdiction of the state. Secularization involves the transformation of political culture as politically relevant values assume a secular orientation. Nationality and nationalism displace religious notions of political community and secular ideologies develop a legitimating power of their own'.[20]

Orientalist Islam is what the West would like the whole of Muslim world to follow. In some of the universities in Muslim countries a number of Muslim academics teach Orientalist Islam as they have all qualified from Western universities and this suits the secular governments in those countries. The Muslim who believes in Orientalist Islam finds it very comfortable to live in Western countries.

Conclusion

The sectarian factor seems to have become acute in Britain. The reason for this is that the average Muslim is reacting to the secular context. If he goes to a restaurant, he cannot eat meat because it is not *Halal* (permitted by Islamic law). If his girls are going to a mixed school, he fears that his daughter will become pregnant. If she attends any classes on sex education, he fears the teachers will teach her how to have sex. He fears sending his children to educational institutions because they may indocrinate them with secular values. He does not want the children to watch television because explicit love scenes are sometimes shown. One can go on citing such examples. Such Muslims may seem to have become paranoid about Western culture, society and civilization. Such paranoia is publicly registered in a number of significant ways. Firstly, in clinging to their religion, the various segments of the community have instead clung to their sectarian affiliations. This has then increased intra-sectarian rivalries such as between Wahhabis versus Barelvis or Shi'ite versus Sunnis — which clearly defeats the purpose of being a Muslim, that is, of being a united community. Secondly, their reaction has resulted in a crisis of identity. In order that they should not be lumped together with the dominant culture some have sported a beard, others hijab, while various styles of clothes, scents (ittar), beads, etc. have been used to proclaim one's different identity. Normally such manifestations would be unnoticed in Muslim societies. But when it is done here as a badge to proclaim oneself as a Muslim, the style of dress or fashion is labelled 'Islamic' and those who are not doing so are considered less than Islamic, then the reaction borders on paranoid attitudes. Such reactionary attitudes should not be confused with the old-timers who wears his *shalwar-khameez* (cultural dress from Pakistan) because he feels comfortable in it and not out of insecurity and he does not expect others to do so. Thirdly, another way such paranoia is exhibited by Muslims is adherence to rituals. When such Islamic rituals become an end in themselves than the world view of Islam is lost. Islam then has been made into an elephant. Some have grabbed its trunk, others its legs, tail or ears, and each thinks that they are in sole possession of Islam and have no idea of its totality. Rituals when they become an end in themselves lose their dynamics. When they are a means to an end, they are Islamic. So with all the prayers being offered every day in the mosques in Britain and many other rituals of Islam being followed, how is it that Muslims have not become an *Ummah* (united Islamic community)? The answer lies in the fact that they have become reactionary.

The reactionary form of Islam exposes a sense of insecurity. It does not lead to the formation of a community. It may not show lack of the depth of faith but lack of understanding of the spirit of the faith. Any Muslim can pray five times a day but if he or she does not have a strong sense of belonging with the community then they lack an understanding of the spirit of the faith. In fact the Prophet's understanding of community (*Ummah*) was such that he stated: 'Muslims are like one body; if one part of the body hurts, the whole becomes sick'. The message here is clear: the principle of unity is not only essential but crucial to the survival of the Muslim community in Britain. In an anti-Islamic society, a divided Muslim community plays into the hands of those who seek to keep it weak. Disunity is suicidal to the survival of Muslims in Western societies for a divided community is weak and vulnerable to attacks.

Chapter 4 *Leadership Role Models*

Leadership is the most important variable in the development of a community. Without leadership, a community is like a ship without a rudder. This is not the situation characterizing the Muslim community in Britain. On the contrary, if anything, the situation is at the other extreme. It is saturated with leadership. Particularly in the area of Islamic leadership there is no dearth. It seems that everyone has rediscovered his or her faith. Yet the tragedy is that the Muslims don't seem to be any nearer to a holistic understanding of Islam. On the contrary, as explained in earlier chapters, the mushrooming of leaders within the community is due to reactionary Islam. The result is that such leadership is at odds with itself, and such a situation is just as disastrous as if the community had no leadership.

There can be nothing worse than when the leaders of the community are all fighting with each other for a wide variety of vested interests. It is ultimately the community that suffers and leaves the young no wiser about Islam. All the three factors of class, ethnicity, and sectarianism, explained in the previous chapter have produced Islamic leadership which is not appropriate to the community. The irony is that all the leaders say that they are acting in the interests of Islam and the Muslim community. Let us consider three models of Islamic leadership currently found in the Muslim community: (1) petro-dollar; (2) professional; and (3) traditional. These categories should not be treated as mutually exclusive for they can overlap. But in general the role models differentiate them in view of their different sources of working for Islam.

Petro-Dollar Leadership
One of the major factors leading to the transformation

of Arab society in the Middle East is oil. According to a well-known Middle Eastern sociologist 'the traditional Bedouin diet of milk, dates and meat has been supplemented by Uncle Ben's converted rice and canned food...There are signs of increased divorce, alcoholism and drug use among the younger generation of Bedouins'.[1] Such rapid changes in the traditional ethical structure of, for example, Saudi society has created disaffection among both the old and the young. The 'moral hypocrisy of ruling elite' has been under particular focus by the young Islamic militants' 'while the ruling elite has tried to spread wealth to all corners of the kingdom'.[2] Such wealth has not only been splashed over the Saudi kingdom but also abroad, particularly to Muslims in Europe. In order to appear Islamic the Saudi ruling elite has paid large sums to upgrade their Islamic image. In Britain over 800 mosques are funded by Saudi Arabia, and many Imams and others are directly funded by the Saudi embassy. The Saudis 'are estimated to have poured £50 million into Britain over the past decade'.[3] The reason for such investment is clear for, in the words of Haroon Jadhakhan, editor of the *Muslim Chronicle,* 'the Saudis finance the mosques to get their own point of view put across. If the Imams don't do this they won't get their pay packets. They can't criticise the government because if they do, they will be sacked'.[4] Petro-dollar leadership is the mouthpiece of foreign countries, not of Islam. Most Muslims and non-Muslims may have heard about petro-dollars but not about its politics. It has created changes in the social structures of Muslim countries giving rise to the vested interests of those who hold the reins of power, business or the armed forces. Power elites in the above-mentioned arenas have become rich while the poor have remained poor. In the 1960s, the danger they faced was from Communism and countries such as Iraq, Iran, Turkey, and some others even had Communist political groups and parties but all such groups failed to rise because they lacked grass-root basis. Instead Islamic groups arose and could quickly build a basis among the masses because their social culture was Islamic.

The social culture of the elites was Westernized for in their efforts to modernize their countries they had become Westernized and all forms of secular ideas were imported into the Muslim societies. The most powerful Western idea which was imported because it suited the vested interests of the political elites was that religion was separate from politics. In other words Islam was treated like Christianity and relegated to the mosques and reduced to a set of rituals like *Salah* (prayers). But the challenge was taken up by a number of Islamic groups and individuals in various countries, and the ruling elites sensing the threat from this quarter since it had grass-root influence moved quickly to crush them in the 1960s in countries like Egypt and Iran. Some were hanged, assassinated or exiled, and their movements banned. But they became martyrs and their writings and resistance had spread their influence far across their borders. During the 1970s Islamic groups posed a serious threat to the state and the ruling elites. Islam rather than communism or socialism became the force which state authorities began to fear.

Three strategies were then used by some of the oil-producing ruling elite dynasties. First, oppression and tyrannizing Islamic groups increased. It is beyond the purpose of this book to focus on those Islamic groups. It is sufficient to state that in many Muslim countries, irrespective of whether they were oil producers or not, the persecution of Muslim groups started. Some of the prominent countries were Saudi Arabia, Egypt, Iran, Turkey, Algeria, Tunisia, Indonesia, the Gulf States and Iraq. Muslim leaders and groups were jailed, tortured or murdered.

Second, the above tactic was not considered enough to

eradicate Islam. If one leader was killed or murdered, two others emerged in their place. The threat was constant and as such it was thought that revolutionary Islam had to be replaced with what has come to be labelled as 'official Islam'. This Islam legitimized the status quo of the ruling elites and their power. The arms of the various religious establishments were twisted and their heads replaced to do the bidding of the state and the ruling elites. Some new organizations were opened who would fund groups who followed 'official Islam'. Their main task was to produce Islamic literature twisting and distorting its interpretation in a manner where state power was not threatened by the Islamic threats. Various institutions, like the *Rabita al-Alam al-Islami* (World Muslim League) in Saudi Arabia, funded political parties, like the Jamaat-i-Islami of Pakistan, to produce the literature of Islam which suited and reinforced the line of 'official Islam'. The threat envisaged by the ruling elite suffered its hardest blow when one of the Islamic movements led by Ayatollah Khomeini toppled the monarchy of Iran in 1979. This created fear among the Saudi monarchy and other dynastic elites in the Gulf States who sought to project their kingdom as Islamic.

Thirdly, the Islamic revolution in Iran had also shown that a revolution could be devised and activated from abroad. Ayatollah Khomeini himself was exiled in 1964 from Iran but he landed back in Iran triumphant as its Islamic revolutionary leader. This established the fact that countless Iranian students, intellectuals, and Ulama abroad in Europe and the USA had played an instrumental role in activating the Islamic revolution in Iran. The elite dynasties started to find those individuals and groups of Muslims abroad who could support 'official Islam'. It is this factor that gave birth to petro-dollar leadership, which can be located in Britain and the USA and other countries of the West. It created the Islamic entrepeneur who had emigrated in search of a a livelihood in Britain. But with this need of petro-dollar countries, such entrepreneurs soon found a commodity to sell, i.e. Islam. Such leadership came from a cross-section of the Muslim community ranging from the highly educated to the illiterate.

The forms in which such leadership in Britain manifests itself are easily visible. The criteria of selection for such leadership are not dependent on a knowledge of Islam or even depth of belief but an ability to faithfully tow the line of 'official Islam' explained earlier. Such leaders act as agents of sponsor countries to create an Islamic image of their sponsors. They also perform the task of recruiting new talent in support of 'official Islam'.

Such leaders can easily be spotted by their lack of criticism of the oppression and tyranny of their foreign government sponsors. Whatever may be happening in the sponsoring country they turn a blind eye to it or whitewash it in public. The Rushdie affair exposed a conflict in this area in Britain. Since countries like Saudi Arabia had not been seen to be very critical in exerting pressure on the British government to ban the book, their agents of 'official' Islam in Britain were under tremendous pressure not to criticize them. Not only the Saudi government but also their agents were discredited in many segments of the Muslim community, and they have suffered in terms of image. The agents dealt in trivial issues for they could not afford to have their funding sources dry up as a result of public comments or actions disliked by their sponsors. Another example was Iraq's invasion of Kuwait. The Saudi ruling elite panicked and invited US troops into their country. This infuriated the Muslim community in Britain for there were no guarantees that such non-Muslim troops would not be going to the forbidden cities of Makka and Madina. The Saudi government had to put a stop to it. So *Darul Ifta* (Ministry of

Islamic Guidance) recalled its agents from the petro-dollar, professional and traditional leaders to a three-day conferance where these 'leaders of British Muslims have been ordered to toe the Saudi line in the Gulf crisis or risk losing financial support'.[5] They also printed pamphlets justifying the presence of US troops.

One very important function of petro-dollar leadership is to disseminate information about the authenticity of 'official'Islam. This is done in a number of ways: (1) The leaders hold a number of functions and conferences where such messages are propagated through speeches. (2) For the young their youth groups will hold summer camps — an idea taken over from the USA where it has been very popular. The minds of the youth are brainwashed by 'official' Islamic doctrines. (3) The leaders also publish a number of books and magazines. Some publishing houses are funded by their sponsors. Their books and magazines will have glossy covers and are expensively produced for funds are not a problem. The really serious problem lies with the messages given through this literature of 'official' Islam. It is not critical of any Saudi ruling elites nor is it in any way politically concerned with serious issues plaguing the Muslim world. On the contrary, it encourages sectarian views and is critical of countries which oppose the Islamic ideologies of their sponsor countries. They may speak of Jihad (struggle), or revolution – but all these arguments seem hollow. People tend to blame the Imams for sectarian views, but it is the petro-dollar leaders who are mainly responsible for the intellectual legitimation of sectarianism.

Petro-dollar leaders may consider themselves to be 'fundamentalist' but they are really funded Muslims. They have sold Islam at a price and, as such, their Islam is compromising. It does not attempt to change the conditions prevailing in their countries of origin. Such leadership has merely spread discord in the Muslim community in Britain. This leadership has not been able to provide direction to the Muslim community or show any substantial achievement which the Muslims can be proud of. On the contrary, they have enriched themselves in the name of Islam and left the community to fend for itself. The reason why they have not worked for the community is because they do not depend on the Muslim community. Their funds, as stated above, come from foreign governments, and Islam for them has become a fruitful entrepeneurship while the masses have suffered. Petro-dollar leadership therefore has lost all credibility due to its mercenary nature and cannot lead the Muslim community in Britain.

Professional Leadership

The prospect of becoming a leader of men or of a community offers a great attraction to men in various professions. Such Muslims may be doctors, medical or in other Islamic or non-Islamic subjects, dentists, barristers, businessmen, lecturers, etc. who have aspired to acquire Islamic leadership roles. The question is: why have they tried to become leaders? It is not enough to argue that they are any more Islamic than the factory worker. The reason for this leadership lies in their education and personal egos.

Such leadership is not the creation of petro-dollars although many are tempted by them. It is mainly a creation of their education which in a community, lacking high educational qualifications such as doctorates, created a vacuum of such leadership roles. The majority of Muslims, as stated in earlier chapters, were illiterate and migrated in search of earning a livelihood. This immediately created a division between the educated and the uneducated leading to the creation of the professional status-elite. The uneducated looked up to the educated for help and advice. In some cases, those with a little education — as a result of which they were able to speak more English than others — gave them a slight edge over the uneducated. Many such persons have become 'community' leaders.

The second reason which has prompted such leadership to emerge is the personal egos of such professionals. Some of them by virtue of their profession are well placed. They are not interested in the lower classes or their problems. But in their profession they have not found the satisfaction which has given them any kind of recognition. The need for some form of recognition leads them to search for leadership not in their professions but in the Muslim community. As stated earlier, the uneducated look up to the educated for leading them. The educated, whether they have any knowledge of Islam or not, suddenly find themselves expected to guide the uneducated. Although not motivated by money as in petro-dollar leadership these leaders certainly show more responsibility to the community. But due to the pressing demands of their professions they do not have much time to give to the leadership thrust upon them. They too have failed to lead the community for their service is limited. On the other hand, many professionals who have given up their professions and who are engaged in full-time Islamic work have been tempted by petro-dollars and have joined the ranks of the petro-dollar leadership.

Traditional Leadership
The traditional leadership of the majority of the working class Muslims in Britain is in the hands of the Ulama. The Imams were imported from the country of origin. Most of these Imams are from the Indo-Pakistan subcontinent and often from the villages and *biraderies* of the people who have brought them over here as Imams of the mosques.

The majority of the Imams lack a thorough knowledge of Islam. Their knowledge is limited to the sectarian parameters of the sect they belong to. Such teaching thrives on demeaning the doctrines of other sects, and the result is that two Imams of different sects cannot sit on the same platform. This leadership, myopic in its view, has led to the divisiveness within the Muslim community. Another area where such traditional leadership shows its ignorance is that the leaders do not know anything about the context in which they are resident. They can neither speak the English language nor are acquainted with the socio-political context of the dominating British culture. They cannot then propose any solutions to the problems arising in Britain among the younger generation for their solutions have emanated from their countries of origin.

Traditional leadership has no communication with the younger generation for they cannot provide answers to the questions asked by the latter. British education opens the mind of the younger generation in its schools and universities to think through issues, but when the teenagers put these questions to Imams they cannot get answers because the Imam either is dogmatic or does not know how to reason. Such ignorance in highly industrialized societies neither helps the young nor builds their confidence in traditional leadership.

Traditional leadership is also flawed in Islamic guidance. They have only a ritualistic and literal understanding of their faith. They do not think that rituals have meanings which can have many interpretations. In other words, Imams lack conceptual knowledge. Lacking conceptual knowledge, they cannot see Islam in its wider global context addressing a number of issues that face the world today, from the daily lives of the people to international politics. The result is that the solutions traditional leadership proposes to problems are either escapist or obscurantist in nature.

It is here that the Ulama as a group have failed the Muslim community in Britain. It has kept Islam on a simplistic level. By knowing the *Kalimah* (creed of the faith), prayers and the Arabic language, recitation of the Qur'an does not guarantee an understanding of the totality of the faith.

Leadership of the community was thrust upon the Ulama. In the villages where they lived they would have been under the thumb of the District Officers or the landlords. In Britain the scene changed completely. The Imam came to be in charge of not only mosques but also communities. He was offered a platform for addressing congregations of believers. The older generation were their only followers and they were subservient because their level of understanding and knowledge of Islam was even lower than that of the Imams.

The Imams were the only persons who, as the equivalent of priests, were often called upon to perform numerous other Islamic activities like marriages, funerals, and remembrances of the dead relatives. Here again they gained a lot of influence among various members of the community, some important, some rich, and were paid for the services mentioned. They found themselves indispensable to the Muslim community. The Imams themselves gained a sense of importance when members of the indigenous communities like headmasters, teachers, police officers and local authority officials called on them for various services. In his country of origin an Imam was a nobody and now he is somebody. This again gave him an exaggerated sense of importance of his own role. In all fairness, there is no doubt that such traditional leadership has rendered one invaluable service to the Muslim community. It has established mosques and help in their caretaking. In this sense it has served the needs of the community more than other leaders. However, it has not been sufficiently competent enough to raise the community's level of thinking to impact with issues outside the mosques in the society at large. Nor has it created unity in the community due to blind adherence to their sectarian loyalties.

Conclusion

The leadership of the Muslim community has failed its community. Petro-dollar leadership has sought its inspiration in money, professional leadership has sought the solace of its ego and traditional leadership has sought to raise the profile of its own sect. The Imams may have tended the mosques but have lost understanding of what the function of mosques has been in Islam. Instead the mosques have been turned into medieval sectarian fortresses.

Since the Muslim community has been primarily illiterate and uneducated, there was a vacuum of leadership everywhere and it often thrust itself upon persons who could not render selfless service. In terms of accountability nobody has been responsible. Vested interests of leaders have therefore taken off in tangential ways dividing the community and leaving its interests untended. Consequently, the Muslim community has local and not national leadership.

Chapter 5

Muslim Political Participation

The role models of community leadership which have been explained in the preceding chapter have failed the Muslim community. A number of reasons were given for their failure. This chapter will explore one major reason for their failure as well; this is in relation to the political system of Britain. The leadership has been so occupied owing to their in-fighting that they have not made any attempt to exert an influence on the political system. What the Muslim leadership has not realized is that, when any community is without any political power in the society it is resident in, it is at the mercy of those in power. Without political clout it is open to attack from any quarter. There are two ways in which such political protection can be acquired. First, the political elite (MPs, ministers, etc.) in power can themselves think about an injustice or inequality suffered by a minority and eradicate it through legal protective measures. They may not always know in advance which laws may be necessary but when they do come to realize a problem, they can do something about it. Second, it is up to the community suffering an injustice to start exercising political clout and get such laws passed. This can only be done through political participation at the national level. However, because of the situation in which it finds itself, the Muslim community has become isolated.

These two options are analysed in this chapter. The status quo of the Muslims political scene will be looked at through the level, structure, context and concentration of Muslim political participation in Britain.[1]

The Level of Political Participation
Although Muslim participation through voting takes place at both local and national levels, it is limited, and the three

factors of class, ethnic and sectarian pointed out in Part I of the study still continue to affect Muslim political participation.

On the local level Muslims have been fighting with local authorities for the redress of grievances on a number of issues. These issues along with the questions they raise have been investigated by Dr J. Nielsen. They are:

1. Burial
   (a) Are particular areas of cemeteries set aside for Muslim burial?
   (b) Are Muslims permitted to inter their dead according to their customs, e.g. with cloth rather than a coffin?
2. Slaughter
   Do Muslims have access to (a) cattle and (b) poultry slaughtered according to their religious requirements?
3. Worship
   Do Muslims in the employ of your local authority have the right to (a) days off on religious festivals and (b) time off for Friday noon prayers?
4. Education
   (a) Is there a policy on the part of the local authority regarding making school facilities available for Muslim religious instruction?
   (b) What is the local authority's practice regarding mother tongue teaching?
   (c) How do school meals make allowance for Muslim dietary rules?
   (d) What is the authority's policy on school uniforms for Muslim girls?
   (e) What is the authority's practice regarding sex education?
   (f) What is the authority's policy on racism and/or multicultural education?
5. Voluntary Schools
   Has the authority been approached regarding the

possibility of establishing a Muslim voluntary school? If so, when? What is the current situation of the approach (rejected, accepted, under discussion)?

6. Planning Permission

(a) What are the authority's policy guidelines on planning permission for mosques and places of private Islamic instruction?

(b) How many mosques are known to be functioning with and without planning permission?

7. Literacy

(a) Does the authority have a literacy programme directed specifically at Asian women; how does it function?

(b) Does the library service have a policy of encouraging Asian language users?[2]

On these issues some authorities have acceded to some demands, others have not. At every step, the Muslim community has had to negotiate for 'Muslim self-determination'.[3]

Even small issues can flare up and Muslims have to fight for their right to redress. The case of the Alavi sisters is significant in illustrating this point. When they started wearing the *Hijab* to Altrincham Grammar School for Girls they were turned away from the school. The issue had been dragging on for a number of months when the girls decided to challenge the school for a decision. When the issue was brought before the school governors, they fearing that another issue might arise, granted the sisters the right to wear the *Hijab* in school.[4] The girls in question in this case had to challenge the school single-handedly. In another case, where a headmaster refused to allow a Muslim boy to wear a beard in his school in Peterborogh, community support was mobilized and the boy was allowed to keep his beard. Both these cases show that without challenging the system people's legitimate rights cannot be gained.

Mobilization of Muslims is essential at every step. When it was explained to them that, if they were elected as school governors, Muslims would have more say in the education of their children, a number stood for election and actually became school governors. However, while mobilization on the local level has given the Muslim community some experience, on the national level their track record is very weak.

The reason for this is that most Muslims suffer from a very low self-image of themselves. Coming from the former colonies of the Raj their attitudes towards the structure of authority have been very deferential not only in their countries of origin but also in Britain where their leadership has not done anything to raise their self-image. But their low self-image does not relate to Islam. Their relationship to Islam raises their self-images. It is the one sacred aspect of their lives which no one is allowed to desacrilize. Any desacrilization can lead to defiance. This was manifested in the Rushdie affair.

In the Rushdie affair Muslims employed tactics which are recognised forms of political protest but of which they hardly had any experience. Particularly in the burning of the Rushdie book they gave vent to their pent-up anger hardly knowing the history of book burning in Nazi Germany and elsewhere. Some of their tactics in the Rushdie affair were:
1. Complaining to the authorities.
2. Marching in peaceful processions.
3. Communicating the meassage to the media.
4. Burning the Rushdie book in public demonstrations.
5. Debating the question in conferences.
6. Appealing to Muslim countries.
All these responses have given a cross-section of the Muslim community its first lesson in politicization and raised their level of political conciousness from the local to the national

level.

The Structure of Participation

The structure of political participation in the British political arena is very clear. It is a democratic structure in which people are elected to local authorities and parliament through political party structures. Muslims, on the other hand, are not organized. Their way of participation is still based on rural practices from their country of origin. This is to vote on the basis of block votes — through either the *biraderi* linkage or other cultural/sectarian factors. The result is that, in Muslim majority-dominated areas, Muslim votes are divided. In Britain the Muslims realised that in order to wield some control they will have to have political power. Out of desperation and the political conciousness raised by the Rushdie affair they reacted by starting a political party, launched in July 1989, which is the Islamic Party of Britain (IPB). Its objectives are as follows:

1. To present issues both political and social to the British people in the light of the Divine guidance of the Qur'an and Sunnah.

2. To present a viable political, economic and social alternative to the British people.

3. To lobby for political support from the political parties and the government for the needs of the Muslim people.

4. To establish the teaching and the practice of Islam within Britain and Islam's voice within British politics.

5. To establish leadership and unity within the Muslim community here, and a sense of direction and purpose in living in this country.

6. To defend the rights of Muslims throughout the Muslim world and establish solidarity with other Muslim countries and communities living under non-Muslim rule.

7. To actively confront media bias and distortion of issues.

8. To establish regular regional and national rallies/

seminars to call people to Islam and participation in action through support or membership.

9. To promote mutual aid services to its members (interest-free banking facilities, enterprise support, legal indemnification, health care plan etc.).[5]

The IPB was criticized by a number of Muslims on different grounds. Dr. Zaki Badawi of the Council of Imams and Mosques observed that the party was run by 'converts with a few roots'.[6] Dr. Syed Pasha of the Union of Muslim Organizations thought that the party was 'counter-productive' and the Muslims could be represented better through the existing parties. *New Life,* an Asian newspaper, commented that the convert leadership would not understand the real problems of Asians as 'racism which mars the daily lives of most Asians has little relevance for the leaders of the Islamic party'. Such a party was a step which would make the Muslims opt out of the system 'which oppresses us and marginalises ourselves even further', and the party would be 'considered a backward step for our communities'.[7] The party's leaders, half of whom were converts, rationalized against such attacks by stating that 'people can't tell us to clear off back from whence we came, which is the reaction a lot of Muslims receive when they try to raise issues of concern'.[8]

While the intention of the founders may be good, such objectives are out of touch with the context of social reality. Similarly the IPB manifesto seems to be naive when it states that 'believers' 'are those with whom people's lives, wealth and dignity are secure...who when powerful, forgive easily and are generous in appropriate ways'. Does it imply that there are no believers from other faiths who cannot act in a similar manner? If so, then what is so unique about this manifesto? These questions are not meant to discredit the IPB but merely to show that one should not be obscurantist in one's thinking. Failures can only result in the party becoming a laughing stock. The situation would become even more complicated if a number of such foreign-funded Islamic parties were to mushroom and their objectives contradicted each others. Just like petro-dollar leadership they would be fighting each other depending on the political objectives of their paymasters. The result would not only divide Muslim votes and never result in success against the opposition but also would confuse the Muslims further about decisions of who is right and who is wrong. This reactionary attitude reflects an 'escapist syndrome' which has characterized Muslims particularly from the Indo-Pakistan subcontinent, when various religious groups retreated rather than declare Jihad against the British colonialists who had taken over the country. They did not achieve anything. Instead it was the nationalists like Muhammad Ali Jinnah who carved out the state of Pakistan.

The path of participation in the political parties is not easy. For example, a study has shown that there are structural obstacles of racism which operate within the political parties from 'crude racism' through to 'unconscious racism', 'ethnocentricity' and 'double standards'.[9] The study also observes that 'there is more black involvement in the parties than many people assume, but the involvement is patchy. It varies considerably between and within parties but is still proportionally lower then the involvement of whites. Black people within the parties are less likely to hold party or elective office, yet the number of black councillors and candidates has been rising steadily. Those whom the parties see as representing black people may be seen by black people as thoroughly unrepresentative. The party members who appear to give the greatest encouragement to black involvement may prove the greatest obstacle to giving black people equal opportunities in the parties and the parties themselves, in the name of racial equality, may actually exploit black people. Above all, while the parties and black people generally agree that there should be more involvement, there is little clear idea what either side should realistically hope for as a result.[10]

Furthermore, Muslims have not yet transcended their kinship and cultural ties as studies of Pakistani voting behaviour proved in the 1970 in by-elections in Rochdale. Muhammad Anwar observed that the Pakistani voting pattern was still determined by *biraderi* links. The fact that there was a switch of Pakistani votes from the Labour Party to another party was because Labour had supported India during the 1971 Indo-Pakistan war.[11]

Muslim community leaders therefore have to think clearly on the issue of political participation whether the community should lead itself towards marginalization of itself or they should penetrate the mainstream political parties. According to one analyst from Bradford University, a number of constituencies in Britain have a high percentage of Muslim voters as in Rochdale, in the Sparkbrook and Small Heath constituencies of Birmingham, in the west and north constituencies of Bradford, Luton South and Bethnal Green in London. The number of Muslim voters will increase, by say 1992, as the younger generation reaches voting age. But 'to maximise that potential requires considerable finesse. If a Muslim minority – and Muslims are still a minority in every constituency – were to make extensive demands as a condition of its support that tactic could prove counter-productive. A member of parliament might conclude that a number of votes lost by refusing Muslim demands would be less than the non-Muslim votes gained as a consequence of publicising Muslim demands and publicly refusing them'.[12] The analyst concluded that Muslim 'interests are still best served through the established parties'.[13]

The Muslim community has not yet learnt how to

approach the British political system. It lacks the political experience which is practised by other communities like the Jews. The implicit trust placed on the state and its political elites by the Muslim community has not paid off. Working in the anti-Islamic context the Muslims have to adopt various sophisticated ways of political participation. Approaches through recognized strategies offer the best options.

Participation Strategies
The recognized strategies are as follows:
1. Active participation in local councils.
2. Active participation in British political parties at local and national levels.
3. Active work with political parties to learn mobilization and participation tactics.
4. Articulation of views on political agendas on issues which may not be related to Islam or Muslim community affairs but are of national importance, e.g. race relations, foreign affairs and secular issues.
5. Attempts to get Muslim candidates into various political positions.

The above strategies are easier said than done, and require a shrewd knowledge of the political system.

Furthermore, the concentration of the members of the Muslim community is limited. It is mainly from the business and professional elites. Most of them are secular and as such have not been able to wield any influence or political clout. The main reason is that they have limited political skills, perhaps because Muslims lack command of the English language and oratory powers, lack sophisticated and incisive reasoning as well as lack grass-root influence, networks and organization. In other words they lack political education. Such political education should be imparted to the younger generation of Muslims. But there are no institutions opened by the Muslims where such political education can be imparted. Mere teaching of simplistic and ritualistic Islam will not teach political education.

The issues facing Muslims are real and can be solved in the local and national political arenas of Britain. Three examples will explain the point: (1) the Education Reform Act 1988; (2) voluntary aided schools; and (3) single sex schools.

Education Reform Act 1988
The education Reform Act 1988 made it compulsory on all county schools to hold daily Christian worship (Assembly) and provide Christian religious education. For Muslim parents there were four options: (1) to let their children get Christian religious education; (2) to withdraw their child from the school, which they could do under the Act; (3) where Muslims are in the majority, to negotiate for alternative collective worship (Assembly) or Islamic religious education and let the local education authority pay for it; and (4) where children are in the minority, to hold negotiations for Islamic assembly and religious education at the community's expense.[14] The point to be emphasized here is that none of the above can be achieved without political negotiations. The very fact that such an Act was passed exposes the government's internal colonialism because it never thought that Britain was a multicultural society.

Voluntary Aided Schools
There are many voluntary aided schools which belong to the Christian and Jewish faiths. Muslims have also been asking for them because they do not have voluntary aided schools, and Muslims like Yusuf Islam have been in the forefront of this struggle. In all respects the Muslims are entitled to them by rights — the same rights which grants them to other denominations. The fear below the surface is: 'would state funded schools serve to encourage Islamic fundamentalism, religious and cultural separation?[15] If this

dilemma confronts the authorities it is a reflection of their anti-Islamic attitude. But the fight is a political one according to the law which grants to one religion what it does not grant to another religion. The Muslims as equal citizens of the state have to demand their rights. It is a right which the Muslims have to take advantage of: either it is granted to none or granted to all.

The voluntary-aided schools can raise many questions which have been pointed out by Halstead when he observes 'The call for Muslim voluntary-aided schools, however, is only part of a much broader issue: the problem of what education for Muslims should be like in a situation where they are a minority community in a Western democracy. This broader issue raises a number of questions, such as what implications a belief in Islam has for education, especially in the contemporary world; what account should be taken of these implications by the authorities when the Muslims form a minority community; how far Islamic values are compatible with those of the broader community in the UK; what rights the Muslim community has within a Western democracy; and what attitude Muslims should have to concessions which are made to their community, especially when such concessions only partially respond to their wishes or demands. These questions can only be resolved by reference to fundamental concepts such as educational accountability and the aims of education, community, personal and social identity, the nature of commitment, truth, belief, religion, secularism, culture, tradition, pluralism, integration, tolerance, neutrality, automony, rationality, justice, freedom and democracy.[16] But before this or any other problems are resolved, it is essential to acquire the right, first, for the establishment of voluntary-aided schools.

Single Sex Schools
Single sex schools are again the right of Muslims. Once

more, the arguments again should be political and not Islamic. The government has given the right to parents to choose schools on racial grounds.[17] By the same criteria, parents do not want their children to study in mixed schools so parents have the right to send their daughters to schools which are exclusively for girls. Muslims are not asking for Muslim girls schools. The question here of the right for Muslim parents to choose and if so Muslim parents have to fight for that right again in the political arenas.

Conclusion

Political participation is very essential for the survival of Muslims in Britain. Training within the political arena and the community institutions is nesessary, and as yet Muslims are lacking in both. Muslim politics have focused more against each other. The politics of the Muslim community are like feudal politics reflecting the political culture of their countries of origin. They are all chiefs with no Indians. Most of these leaders who would never have had any political voice in their own countries as landless peasants dominated by their landlords find the British context very conducive. It has given them importance and attention, and so community leaderships have become a game to be played against each other. Class, cultural and ideological ties all play their subtle roles in such leadership. But the role definition of leadership in the British political arena is another thing. The rules of the game are different, and Muslims have a chance of success if they grasp the system.

But they need training in political education and political participation, the most important areas being:
1. Formation of Muslim pressure group organizations with a view to engaging in organized lobbying.
2. Formation of specialized agencies by Muslims on specialized areas such as futuristic studies and polling Muslim opinions. All such organizations should draw

funding from their own resources and not from foreign governments. Foreign funding produces foreign mouthpieces which do not address the problems confronting the Muslim community in Britain. Instead it gives the foreign views of the communities problems in Britain.

3. Formation of a national think-tank for framing the social policy of Muslims on various issues confronting the community. It should have the potential to get the consensus of Muslims and build networks with political/religious/social organizations.

4. Political training should be given to the younger generation in the Muslim organizations. These should discuss issues irrespective of whether they are religious or secular.

5. Strategic planning which has to focus more on participation lobbying and pressure group tactics.

Chapter 6 Mosques and Centres

There are over 1,000 mosques in Britain and their number is increasing. Most of the mosques are in terraced houses and are small. Others are purpose-built and are large, and are very beautiful. But apart from the traditional dome in the Islamic architectural style, all other aspects of a mosque are in the Western architectural style.

The building of so many mosques in Britain however does not reflect the fact that Islam is on the increase in Britain. *The Islamic Cultural Centre* in London correctly observes that the 'mosques in Britain have become a battle ground for power politics...It is pointless to conceal that within the last few years most of the trouble and discord have stemmed from the attitudes of some of the Ulema and Imams and these have been the reason for many of the most unpleasant scenes witnessed in the brief history of the Muslims in the United Kingdom. In some cases the troubles have escalated to such an extent that the police have had to enforce the closure of the mosques'.[1] Such an attitude from the central institution of Islam not only shows a lack of understanding of Islam but also a lack of commitment to it.

Mosque politics has a place of its own in the Muslim community. The mosque has become an instrument of sectarianism. This sectarianism is vented against other Muslim sects. The mosque acts as a focus of power of one sect against another. As a focus of power the mosque is more powerful than Muslim organizations for it operates at grassroot level. It also offers a platform for those aspiring to become leaders rather than to be of service to Islam.

Furthermore, cultural and national factors in addition to sectarian, ethnic and class factors, are also at the centre of mosque politics. The sectarian level is easy to spot for in every city of Britain there will be a number of mosques catering to the needs of each sect. One researcher observed that 'despite Islam's denial of recognising national boundaries, mosques in Birmingham have been created on an ethnic/national basis'.[2] Consequently the city has separate mosques for Punjabis, Mirpuris (people from Azad Kashmir), Pathans, Bangladeshis, Yemenis and Gujratis.

There is nothing wrong with these groups having their own mosques, but it would have Islamic legitimation if they were built in healthy competition in order to make one mosque which was better than all the others provided there was unity. Instead the truth is the reverse, for these mosques built for Islam soon change their objectives and work against each other's interest, and there is active hostility between them. This is the pattern found in every city.

Another reason why the mosques have become divided is due to petro-dollars. As petro-dollars have divided Muslim leadership the mosques have not been immune to such foreign influence. They have sold their faith for petro-dollars. The Saudis, as explained in Chapter 4, have been a major source of funds and have often made large sums of money available for dispersal to mosques. Such is the inducement of money that 'many independent mosque committees had joined the Council of Mosques on the hope that it would promise them Saudi finance'.[3] Petro-dollar control over mosques has become the major strategy in order to de-Islamicize them. No money is given without strings attached. Once the mosque is a recipient of petro-dollars it tows the line of official Islam. One way to spot such mosques is that they are often purpose-built and are very beautiful to look at. An example of this is the 'President Saddam Hussein Mosque' in Birmingham. It was built with more than a £1·5 million donation by the Iraqi leader. It is not surprising that the mosque committee 'has an interest in the Iraqi

President's continued good health' because he has promised them another lump sum to build a cultural centre.[4] This is just one example but others are funded by other Muslim countries.

There is no doubt that purpose built mosques are beautiful. But that is about all they possess thereby fulfilling the truth of a tradition of the Prophet which stated: 'A time will come over my Ummah when they will vie with one another in the beauty of their mosques. Then they will visit them but little'.[5] The mosques may have gained in architectural beauty but have lost in religious depth.

Yet another way in which the mosques have been controlled is by some persons or groups who have taken over the mosque committee. For many Muslims who are on mosque committees it offers them prestige. If that is the motive for joining the mosque committees, then it not only shows a defective understanding of Islam but also explains why the Muslim community has not benefited from the services of mosques. As Nadeem Ahmad, a young sociologist, correctly observes: 'The majority of mosques have become the personal property of select committees who have complete disregard for criteria other than their own'.[6] Moeen Yaseen, a young educationalist, further reinforces the observation by stating that 'In the UK, mosques are classified as charitable religious organizations serving the interests of the Muslim community and Islam. They are run by trustees and a management committee on a voluntary basis. There appears to be an alliance and trade-off between the interests of secularists and religious leaders. A balance of power of two power-broking elites who are mutually interdependent. The status quo is located in Pakistani culture. In rural societies in the developing world the *Biraderi* based political culture has been enmeshed with business interests which ensures a tight grip on community institutions and leadership. This elite excludes members who do not fit into its criterion. Translating this into practice means that the local ethnic Pakistani establishment operates and functions as a Mafia type system with a Chief or a Chaudhury at the head of this hierarchical structure. Management committees only act to rubber stamp the president-operating on blind loyalty, conformity and deference. This is a system which is inherently authoritarian and dictatorial...Ability, intelligence and specialist knowledge is not required to fit into the political culture and ethos of the organization. Indeed, the prevailing powers are against intellectuals and the educated. Ideologically, there is a promotion of a ritualistic interpretation of Islam. Whilst the Imams from the Indian subcontinent suffice the spiritual, emotional needs of illiterate, semi-literate sectarian *biraderi*-oriented congregations who serve the interests and the linguistic and theological needs of the 'Old Guard.' The administration is technically left to the office bearers – in practice the administrative support structures are weak, ineffective or non existent'.[7] Not until such structural defects in the organization of mosques are eradicated can they then be expected to function constructively for the objectives of Islam.

There are two areas which the mosques have completely ignored – those of women and youth. Very few mosques in Britain have made special provisions for the attendance of women at mosques for prayers or other general functions. Some have distorted Islam and argue that it does not permit women in mosques. Others oppose this view but say that due to limitations of space women cannot be accommodated in the mosques. The mosques have not paid serious attention to this problem.

The youth have also been ignored by the mosques as well. Youths have been flooding the mosques but mosques have not made any effort to organize them. Such organizations could have made youth cells in every mosque and directed them into a number of social activities as well as resolving many of the problems confronting them. It is not surprising when Nadeem Ahmad is critical again and observes: 'The mosques no longer serve the community...They are almost wholly male institutions. No wonder so many British born Muslim women/girls grow up detesting Islam...The mosque is by definition the heart of the community. It has to be multi-dimensional if it is to adequately succeed in harmonizing all the varied elements within the community...I have always felt that mosques should be venues for issues of national importance such as racism, unemployment, the environmental crisis, education, business, the arts and sport. We are being restrictive if we keep them as prayer places alone. The strengths of our mosques can only materialise with their ability to attract a larger audience. They have to utilise all the skills, abilities and talents of the community'.[8] There is no doubt that there is a whole reservoir in the community which is full of talents which can be utilized by the mosques. But this effort has not been made by them to enrich their role in the community.

The older generation lives in a world of its own. It is all very well to write about the ideal role of the mosques as multi-functional, as 'being a place of worship, centre for education, judicial court and centre of government for political and administratives'.[9] But the question then arises that, if the mosque had multi-functional roles, why has it not functioned accordingly. What such Muslims do not question is where does the fault lie and why has it not been rectified by them. One could go on for 100 years saying what the function of the mosque is in Islam, but, if in reality it functions only for prayers and not for other Islamic functions, its function will be limited and it will be counter-productive. It will be counter-productive because the full potential of Islam from its most important institution cannot be realized. The full potential can only be achieved if the Muslim community realizes not only the importance of the mosque but also its multi-functional nature. In Islam the mosque belongs to Allah, and its sanctity cannot be negotiated for petro-dollars by unscrupulous people. The upkeep of the mosque is the responsibility of the Muslim community. If it is in a poor condition, it does not matter for its sovereign sanctity is still intact and has not been bought off by a foreign government or dominated by a class, sectarian or ethnic group. The mosque committee has to be judiciously selected from those who are representatives of the community. If community consciousness does not raise itself to higher levels of thinking, the mosque will always remain a mediocre institution.

The mosque is the most revolutionary institution in Islam. That is the reason why, in many Muslim countries, mosques are supervised by various government departments and ministers to see that 'official' Islam is being preached. No revolutionary anti-establishment messages are permitted, for a congregation which attends a mosque five times a day can easily become revolutionary if the Imam preaches the *Jihad*. The potential of the mosque can be seen in the case of the Rushdie affair. That was the only cause for which mosques have shown some defiance. Many mosques tried to outdo each other in this matter and some Imams from their pulpit even denounced the lack of Saudi Arabian support in banning the book. Here again the important point was that deference to a number of factors such as ethnicity and sectarianism was thrown overboard when it came to an insult on the Prophet Muhammad. The mosque became an instrument of defiance.

Conclusion
The mosques – with few exceptions – seem to have compromised Islam in Britain. This important institution is

being used for personal interests, and the mosque has not been turned into a community centre which is not only alive to the needs of the Muslim community but is also directive. At the moment it is only functioning like the Christian churches — providing a place for prayer and some other rituals such as funerals, marriages, etc. But it has not, as yet, equipped itself to cope with the problems of the Muslim community. The day that the mosques start taking an active stance in the affairs of the Muslim community, then the community will be made strong.

Chapter 7 *Madrassahs and Education.*

Education is a very important aspect of any community, society or civilization. It is related not only to the history of the country but also to the culture, orientation towards the political system and future direction. For example, British education has evolved from its history and not only gears itself to the technological requirements of society in general but also inculcates ideological and socio-political values. These are in line with its political development and secular values. It separates religion from political and morality. Education in Britain, therefore, prepares the individual for a society free from religion. In fact the latest survey of British attitudes towards religion today reflects this. Britain is second only to the Netherlands with people saying that they have no religion. Also Britain is the only country in Western Europe where only 20% per cent regularly attend the church.[1] In such a society where Muslims' children are being raised, it can hardly be expected that they will imbibe any religious values. According to one observer: 'Most parents in the UK send their children to school to learn basic necessary skills, such as reading, writing, science and so on. But, of course, there is a complete culturalization process which underlies the whole system. Every school has a cultural base, from which it derives its goals, objectives and ultimate character, and this is where the process of indoctrination – overtly and covertly – begins. The entire philosophy of State schools is built on *Kufr* (rejection of God and his authority) or, as they would call it 'nationality'. In other words, the assertion of the Supreme Being, as the ultimate source of reality and power in the universe, is viewed from a critical perspective. Even at the best of times 'faith' is presented as a narrow, spiritualistic and rather confusing concept. 'Religions' are grouped together and offered as a hotch-potch optional subject. Therefore the whole identity of the

Muslim character and system of intellectual enquiry is minimalized from the very beginning'.[2] With this status quo the teaching of Islamic education rests with Muslim parents or the Muslim community. But the parents are engaged in earning a livelihood and hardly have the time to give any kind of education. Furthermore the majority of parents are not only illiterate but also ignorant about Islam. Some Muslim families may be able to provide the Islamic knowledge and environment for their children, but such families are the exception rather than the rule. The only way left for Muslims to impart Islamic education to their children is through Islamic educational institutions. In fact this is the reason why such institutions have sprung up in Britain. According to one estimate there are some 350,000 Muslims of school-going age (5–16) who are in need Islamic education and there is a need for 1,000 educational institutions.[3] What then is the state of 'Islamic education and educational institutions?

There are three types of Islamic educational institution for Muslim children. First, there are the mosque schools (Madrassahs), which are attached to the mosques. Second, there are schools run in private homes or in separate places. Third, the primary or secondary schools similar to that of Western education for boys or girls.

According to one estimate there are over 15 schools of the latter type and the waiting list of pupils is growing.[4] Madrassahs, on the other hand, are estimated to be over 500.[5] Islamic education has become big business. But close scrutiny of these educational institutions set up by Muslims does not seem to bring out positive results. A report by Her Majesty's Inspectors on pupils between the ages of 11 and 16 years of age stated that the objective of that particular school was to 'produce women who have faith and who are imbued with Islamic learning and character and are capable of meeting all the economic, social, political, technological, physical, intellectual and aesthetic needs of society semms to have been empty promises'. The Inspectors' report found the school lacking in many aspects and reported that 'the education at present offered makes few if any demands on the girls to be active in their learning...the lack of a balanced curriculum supported by schemes of work, which would provide a framework for learning, is apparent in the low expectations of the staff and the equally low response of the pupils. Few of the girls, if any, can be said to be performing to the extent of their abilities. Indeed, the school has no discernible methods of assessing their abilities'.[6] It is surprising that in a country like Britain such conditions should prevail. While this report makes some important points for evaluating the Islamic education of Muslims. It might be considered biased because it came from the establishment. But a number of Muslims are equally critical of it.

A Muslim teacher who collected data from his own teaching experience at a Madrassah in Lancashire pointed out that space in such schools is cramped; in addition to a lack of skills and abilities, teachers lack a knowledge of English so they cannot communicate properly with children while an inability to speak Arabic properly impairs the reading of the Qur'an. Books and the syllabus are not up to standard. This teacher observes that 'we have a misconception that if someone is *Hafiz* then he is perforce a good teacher. This may be so, but practising Islam and having a background on Islamic ideology and also understanding the new way of teaching and methodology are not the same'.[7] Another very important point raised was about the syllabus which, it is considered, 'needs a lot of rethinking as the children are overloaded with reciting *Dua* and *Kalimas* in Arabic without explaining what they mean...often the syllabus consists of its reading the Qur'an (without understanding a word)'.[8] The plain fact of the matter is that nothing should be taught to children which they cannot understand. If children or young adults cannot understand what they have memorized, how can they defend themselves when their beliefs are attacked by non-believers?

Another Muslim educationalist, Akram K. Cheema, observes that 'Muslim organizations will continue to distrust the state schools and will continue to feel frustrated even if the school trys to meet some of these requirements until they feel that they have some considerable involvement in the decision-making machinery and have some control, power or authority over their children's educational diet. Madrassahs are here to stay in order to meet particular needs and give the faith communities a sense of self-fulfilment. There are grave doubts expressed by almost everyone about the nature of supplementary provision, style of teaching, methods of instructions, disciplinary procedures and many other aspects of the arrangements made at present in most Madrassahs. It may be said that they meet the needs of ritualistic self identity and are serving a purpose almost as a protest but one doubts whether the majority of present supplementary schools come anywhere near meeting the spiritual and actual fulfilment of our Muslim children. Most parents, however, seem to be dissatisfied with the present provision and consider the Madrassah to be far from ideal, but they also believe that improvements will come with experience, time and better resources'.[9]

Another observer points out a further aspect: 'Whether it was accident or design the fact is that in colonial times the ruling power relied on a secularised and thus a neutralised Muslim elite to keep the Muslims in check. The anti-Islamic power structure today relies on this same class of people to do the same thing...if Westernism, or modernism or secularism...has had such a profound influence on Muslims in their own settings, what effect will the context we find ourselves in here today have on our children? Unlike the colonial setting every single Muslim child, is now subject willingly, of course, through the very fact of our being here, to a process which has been hostile to Islam. I am not of course talking about the imparting of pure knowledge which Islam encourages. I am referring to the social, political and economic structures which the system is designed and tailored to serve. Our minds have been so conditioned and our bodies so comforted that the implications of this for us as Muslims have yet to dawn on us...We helplessly deliver our children to *Dar ul Kufr* through the conveyor belt that the education system is'.[10]

The whole mess found in Islamic education is best summed up by Dr Zaki Badawi, Principal of the Muslim College in London, who stated that 'they do not teach children to cope with the realities of life in Britain...parents are incapable of understanding that they have moved to another world'.[11] The Muslims have not learnt how to cope with the fact that they are living in a secular society which will be interested in teaching only its principles. The Muslims have become confused because they do not know how to handle the effect of secular systems on the future of their children. The Muslim case is not helped by their own educational institutions, where in some cases Imams have physically beaten children and the police have had to arrest them.[12]

The method of teaching in the Madrassah could backfire in state schools for no teacher can lift a finger against children; it is obvious that the child is learning through fear in the Madrassah and in the other with patience, skill and logic. At some point when the child grows older, he or she will make a choice between the two and turn against Islamic education. If the child does not make a direct break, then he becomes a hypocrite and pays only lip service to Islamic doctrines. The fact that there are so many Islamic educational institutions in

Britain is not an indicator that Islam is taking root in the country. While the efforts of the Muslims can be appreciated, the defects are numerous and counter productive.

According to the Islamic Educational Trust, the characteristics of Islamic education should be: acquisition of knowledge, imparting of knowledge, inculcating moral values, consideration for public good, development of personality and emphasis on actions and responsibilities. Its ideological orientation should have Tawhid *(unity of God),* *Risalat* (Prophethood), *Akhirah* (Life Hereafter) and *Khilafat* (vicegerent) of man on earth.[13]

Another educationalist, S.A. Ashraf, who has written a number of studies, recognizes that there is lack of integration between secular and Islamic education and considers it necessary that Islamic concepts have to be formulated to 'act as substitutes for secular concepts'. The basic ideas of 'educational metaphysics' that 'the Islamic concept of man has the width and range no other concept of man has. As man can become *Khalifatullah* by cultivating or realizing within himself the attributes of God and as these attributes have a limitless dimension, man's moral, spiritual and intellectual progress is potentially limitless. Secondly...Islam does not put any bar to the acquisition of knowledge. Thirdly education...education must be planned in such a way that it has a balanced interdisciplinary pattern. Fourthly, the spiritual, moral, intellectual, imaginative, emotional and physical aspects of a man's personality are kept in view in establishing the relationship among the disciplines...Fifthly, the development of personality is seen in the context of man's relationship with God, man and nature'.[14]

While the thoughts of such Muslim educationalists are commendable, the problem arises in implementation. Because the Muslim community is not an Ummah, sectarian

61

education and its traditions are being taught in the Madrassah. The understanding of Islam has to be of such a nature that it helps Muslims to cope with the secular system.

Conclusion

The most important factor here is that the Muslims have not as yet realized that they are living in an anti-Islamic secular society. The teaching of Islamic education must be geared to a context in which it is being imparted. The questions which arise in this context and which the Muslim children will have to confront at some point in their lives is not the same as might arise in their countries of origin. In whichever way the Islamic syllabuses are structured they must have such objectives.

1. Islamic education should be investigative and critical. It should be grounded in creating a thinking attitude and not blind acceptance. Blind acceptance of faith in any form is counter-productive. It becomes defensive, reactionary and apologetic, and above all vulnerable to secular arguments. This has been the plight of the whole Muslim world. Muslims living in Britain secular society are living in a more vulnerable position for the whole of society is challenging them at every step.

2. Islamic education must create a strong Islamic identity. Muslims often suffer from weak Islamic identities or suffer from low self-images. The Muslim community has the potential but has not yet developed a strong Islamic identity. They have not understood the *Sunnah* of the Prophet itself in this respect. When he was bestowed with an Islamic identity through divine revelation, he changed the world round him with a permanent Islamic stamp. The Muslim migrants are escapees from their own countries of origin for economic reasons. Their whole Islam places emphasis on ritualism, whereas ritualism forms only a miniscule part of Islam. The Islamic civilization was not created by saying prayers five times a day. Hypothetically

speaking, if all Muslims in the world (estimated to be one billion) say prayers every day, why isn't the Muslim world full of Islamic states with a flourishing Islamic civilization? It is because one's identity is weak or dualized — in which prayers are performed as a ritual not as a prelude to Islamic actions. If the symbolic meaning of prayers is not understood, it becomes a meaningless ritual. A strong Islamic identity means to spiritually liberate oneself from any kind of deferential attitude to secular ideologies of life in the secular context. The sectarian modes of teaching Islam have only inculcated deferential attitudes.

3. Islamic education must open the door of knowledge for both sexes. They must be able to learn any skill, vocation or profession in the secular context and not only be competent but also excel in them. Without excellence the Muslims will never be able to make their mark on history. In early medieval ages the Muslims were the torchbearers of knowledge for Europe. From the expression of their faith, exposition of philosophical issues, experimenting with science and pioneering many fields of knowledge such as art and architecture, they influenced European thinking. Most Muslims have no idea of this rich heritage. It is this tradition of Islamic learning which the Muslims have to pick up. The present-day 'Islamic' education imparted in Madrassahs or other institutions has not comprehended its past heritage and the importance of philosophy and science to Islamic education. They have not even developed a critical view through which they can study their own heritage and analyse where they went wrong and why their lands were colonized.

4. Islamic education must be political. In the democratic system of Britain nothing can be achieved without political knowledge and an awareness of its applications. Every Muslim should receive political education, for religion and politics are not separated in Islam. This does not mean that Muslims have to Islamicize the British political system. On

the contrary, it means becoming thoroughly acquainted with the system and learning the sophisticated techniques needed to deal with secular issues. If Islamic education is not teaching the young the objective and methodology of how to live one's life in a secular system, then it is defective. It must make Muslims politically aware of where their destinies are leaning, are being led, by whom and how they can influence the direction. This issue has been discussed in Chapter 5 and does not need to be expanded further here.

5. Islamic educational research needs to tackle the issues confronting Muslims. The gates of *Ijtihad* (independent reasoning) which Islam permits need to be opened. Since the gates of *Ijtihad* were closed centuries ago, the decline of Islamic law and society has begun. Since no case law confronting new problems arising in the 20th century has arisen, Muslims are therefore confused about many issues. The need for *Ijtihad* is even greater In Britain where probelms arising out of the interaction of the Muslim community within the British context needs solution.

6. Islamic education should be theoretical and practical. Many tall claims are made in Islam that it can do anything in the world. While Muslims may feel good to hear it, the Muslim world does not have much to boast about. Islamic education should therefore bridge the gap between theory and practice.

These are some of the lines suggested for streamlining Islamic education. It is a serious task which has to be taken on board by anyone with a positive understanding of the faith who also knows the secular system well. These questions are relevant to the whole Muslim world.

Chapter 8 *Muslim Organizations*

There are hundreds of Muslim organizations in Britain. In every city there are Muslim organizations which exceed the number of mosques. The majority of these organizations are paper organizations whose founders have either an evangelistic zeal or some ideas which they think ought to be implemented. A few of these organizations are large because they are funded from abroad. They have a board of trustees, and claim charitable status — although their charity has yet to trickle down to the Muslim community. There may be a few exceptions but these organizations are so insignificant that their impact is hardly felt in the Muslim community.

The important question which poses itself is: are these Muslim organizations really serving the cause of Islam in this country? If they were business organizations, such a question would be irrelevant. Since they claim to be Islamic, then the Muslim community has the right to raise such a question. The organizations are accountable to the Muslim community, for Islam is not someone's private property or bank.

One characteristic of Muslim organizations is immediately visible. They are the babies of their founders. Most of the founders of such organizations consider them to be their personal properties even though they are run in the name of Islam. Dr Ahmad Shafaat, who worked in one Islamic organization in Leicester, observed: 'The only Islamic principle they upheld in the Establishment was "obey the Amir", without recognising clearly by words and attitudes that in Islam obedience to the Amir is only meant to be conditional and not unconditional...They (the staff) freely lied, continuously backbited, pursued personal ambitions, played games and competed not in the quality and quantity of work but in staying in favour with the man at the top.

Those who behaved as if obedience to Amir was conditional and also cared for moral principles of Islam were thrown out'.[1] Such attitudes prevail in a number of Muslim organizations. There are a number of reasons for this. In particular, such organizations are nothing more than an outfit for personal publicity or embarking on an ego trip. On paper the committees are nothing more than a group of persons who are there merely to rubber-stamp the policies of the founder. Anyone who flatters the founder is promoted. All this of course is done in the name of Islam.

The characteristic of organizations as pointed out above is nothing more than a reflection of the political parties which prevail in the country of origin of such Muslims. In Pakistan, political parties do not exist to fulfil the demands of the people but to arrange publicity for their founders. The organization by itself does not stand for anything more than to propagate the views of its founders. If the founder dies, such organizations cease to exist although on paper they may continue to do so. Most Islamic organizations do not project Islamic goals but the goals of their leaders under Islamic guises. This is the reason why the spirit of *Shura* (consultation) does not exist. What exists instead is a group of close cliques and, if anybody threatens the views of such cliques, they are removed. Dr Ahmad Shafaat also made another relevant observation in terms of the organizational models followed in Muslim organizations: 'They had two separate models of the Establishment in their minds: an 'Islamic' model derived from the organizational structure of the Pakistani religious-political party to which they belonged and a Western secular model. They moved from one model to another as and when it suited their own ends and wishes. Most of the time they treated the Muslims working there as their employees and not co-workers of Islam. However, if some Muslim staff sometimes felt that, as employees, they should have rights like other employees in Britain, the employees suddenly became 'Muslim brothers' who should be above such rights'.[2] This factor is based on hypocrisy and at the root of it all is money. The larger organizations do not want to share their funds. Just as there is a concentration of power so there a concentration of wealth.

The consequence of this is that Islamic organizations in Britain do not attract the best minds from the younger generations. Only the rejects who cannot find employment elsewhere or have visa problems or are reactionaries and have a strong need to identify with Islam are unfortunately pushed to approach such organizations. They fulfil the conditions of sycophancy and compromising their own opinions. Besides this factor, the job prospects in such organizations are not stable and the pay is not index-linked. So Islamic scholars are not attracted to join them unless they have personal reasons.

The media has investigated some of these organizations but the selection has been arbitrary and many others which exist have not been listed. Those mentioned in one newspaper article are Union of Muslim Organizations, World Muslim League, UK Council of Imams, World Sufi Council, Islamic Council of Europe, World Islamic Mission, the Muslim Institute, UK Islamic Mission, Muslim League, Islamic Cultural Centre and Islamic Guidance Society.[3]

In order to evaluate these organizations there has to be criteria. One thing that the Muslim community in Britain has not realized is that it is not the number but the quality of the organizations that makes them effective. If the quality is poor, there can be hundreds of organizations but they will be ineffective. In Britain just one organization like the Campaign for Nuclear Disarmament (CND) acting as a pressure group can be very powerful. The criteria to evaluate the Muslim organizations are: (1) organizational power and

(2) organizational effectiveness.

Organizational Power

The focus of power within an organization defines the limits to which it can go. If it cannot exercise freedom of choice and action, its powers are limited. From this point of view one can classify Muslim organizations into four types: agent, sectarian, service and independent.

AGENT ORGANIZATIONS

Agent organizations act as agents of their sponsors. The link between the two is that foreign governments or subsidiaries fund such organizations and as such also control the limits to which they can go. Although the agents seem quite free to act, there are invisible constraints on them. For example, the petro-dollar funded organizations cannot say or write about the tyrannous regimes, un-Islamic activities or behaviour of their rulers. They are expected instead to rationalize such behaviour or look the other way. On the other hand, they are expected to be highly vocal or articulate in condemning the enemies of their sponsors.

Agent organizations in the Muslim community also do not enjoy grass-root influence with the ordinary members. Since they are not dependent upon the community for funds (which are of course given to them by their sponsors), they do not work with and for the community. Their facade is to be seen to be working for the community while in reality they are merely serving the interests of their sponsors.

Agent organizations also compromise Islam for their sponsors. They will never be critical of the political, economic or religious policies of the sponsor countries. They know that if they are critical, their funds will soon dry up. Some of these organizations consider themselves as 'fundamentalist' Muslims. The truth is that in reality they are merely funded

Muslims who like the petro-dollar leadership have sold Islam.

A good example of the role of agent organizations can be found in the Rushdie affair. A number of Saudi funded organizations did not support other organizations, because Saudi Arabia did not put itself forward as a vociferous defender of Islam. Its relationship with Britain was considered more important than Islam. The agent organization could not do anything which would embarrass the sponsors.

Another example of agent organizations is their attitude towards other organizations. A noticeable fact about two funded organizations might be that they are not co-operating but are criticizing each other, although the organizational goals of both are the same in principle. To the observer it may seem strange that they should fight. The reason is that the sponsors of the two may be engaged in some form of political conflict with each other. The classic example of such a conflict, which has lasted throughout the 1980s, is that between Iran and Saudi Arabia, the agent organizations of both countries in Britain have never been united over any issue. Through their magazines, newsletters, booklets and books the agent organizations will unite against each other in tearing each other down without realizing that both are in the same position, that is, funded by foreign governments.

Sectarian Organizations
A large number of Muslim organizations are engaged in sectarian work. These are mainly in terms of educational welfare, etc. Here education is given in terms of their own religious doctrines and belief system. The services of such organizations are limited to their sectarian groups. Sectarian organizations also perpetuate sectarianism. In the long run their activities are dividing and not uniting the community.

Such organizations may also strengthen themselves by getting funding like agent organizations. Shia organizations turn to Iran and Wahhabi/Deobandi organizations to Saudi Arabia.

Service Organizations

These organizations are established to provide a specific service. Most of them are inefficient but some have been sincerely devoted to their aim. Charities such as Muslim Aid (London) and Islamic Relief (Birmingham) have been focused only on Muslims. But a newly established charity (under registration), Universal Disasters Fund, was established in Leicester to fund both Muslim and non-Muslim natural and man-made disasters. Other organizations like the Muslim College in London have focused on the training of Imams in Britain and Muslim Law (*Shariah*) Council resolves family and social welfare problems. Others like Muslim Women's Helpline (started by some concerned Muslim women in London) have rendered service to Muslim women. There may be some others worth mentioning and the omission of their names is not deliberate. It is sufficient to state that the scope of service organizations for youth, women, social welfare, etc. is vast but few selfless workers are found.

Independent Organizations

Independent Organizations are those organizations which are not funded by foreign governments. Money is raised through the personal resources of its organizers. They are therefore totally independent and free from control. There are few (if any) independent organizations. They are in fact the organizations of the future, which are above foreign domination (agent organizations) or sectarian controls (sectarian organizations). Furthermore, both the agent and sectarian organizations propagate reactionary Islam. Muslim organizations with strong research orientation, strategic thinking and knowledge of Western contexts also are few, if any. The Muslim Community Studies Institute at Leicester is one such independent organization with those credentials.[8]

Organizational Effectiveness
Evaluating Muslim organizations in terms of their effectiveness is an important question. Two factors need to be addressed. First, if they are to be effective,how should they be so? Secondly, should they be effective towards the Muslim community or to British society, or both? To treat the second question first, it is obvious that the Muslim organizations should be effective in their own community as well as in British society so that bridges can be built and inroads made into the latter. Organizations do not live in a vacuum but within British society. But both the agent and sectarian organizations are incapable of doing this. The agent organizations serve the foreign countries while sectarian organizations serve their own sects. Each keeps their own vested interests first and not that of the Muslim community.

In terms of the effectiveness of Muslim organizations towards British society the results are appalling. Most of the organizations have been engrossed so much within their own internecine quarrels that they have not been able to concentrate on many other issues needing serious planning and execution. Some of these neglected areas have for example been mission work and publishing, which are briefly surveyed below.

Mission Organizations
Mission work organizations have received considerable amounts of money from foreign organizations and rich business magnates. But they have neither developed any mission work nor done any planning. They have not been able to put forward even a simple case for explaining Islam in

71

attractive terms to the non-Muslims. Most of the mission-orientated organizations like the Tabligi-Jamaat or Islamic Mission may talk of missionary work but have not approached non-Muslims with an evangelistic zeal. Above all, the main thing they lack is suitable missionary workers. Most of the missionary workers who roam the cities in Western countries cannot speak any European language, nor do they have the courage or intelligence to converse with non-Muslims on the subject. Converting a non-Muslim is not a matter of telling him or her to accept Islam because it is better than their religion. It needs convincing skills, sufficient command of the language, knowledge of the other person's religion or ideology, as well as missionary skills. Most of these Muslim mission workers are merely focusing on Muslims where there is the least need for new converts. For the latter Western culture itself is pushing them towards Islam.

Publishing Organizations

Muslim publishing organizations have not as yet woken up to their responsibilities. Most of the literature produced has made no impact on anybody. Parallel to such organizations are a number of Western publishers whose works are held in high esteem because of the quality of research work. The reason why Muslim publishing has not been up to the mark is, firstly, because of a ready-made market and lack of any real competition. Parents who want books on Islam for their children will buy any book because they have to. Some have that ready-made market for literature on Islam within their own sectarian populations e.g. the Shi'ites and Sunnis. Secondly, publishers have not had difficulty in raising funds as most of them have been funded by foreign sponsors. The problem has not been in the quality of production but in editorial policy. The contents of the books have been censored. They have produced neither inspirational nor academic books on par with publishers whose Western interpretation of Islam holds the market. In fact the publishing houses have not even offered fair contracts to Muslim writers, many of whom have gone to the Western publishers. Because such publishers have not been under pressure they have felt the need neither to develop distribution and marketing skills nor to cultivate the mainstream market. They have simply failed to rise above the level of sectarian and agent organizations. Some efforts to establish their own Islamic association did not meet with much success because of the same reason. A number of Muslim organizations are media organizations. There are a number of new magazines, newsletters, bulletins, small magazines, etc. but, except for a few, the level of information imparted is simplistic and not analytical. It suffers the same problems as the publishers discussed above due to the constraints of foreign funding and sectarianism. In terms of newspapers referring to Britain *Muslim News* is very good.[5] *The Islamic Times*[6] from The Raza Academy and *Al-Basirah: Bulletin of Islam and Islamic Social Sciences*[7] from the Muslim Community Studies Institute in Leicester are very good for academic analysis.

Conclusion

Muslim organizations have not yet realized that, if such divisions tear them apart, they are only making themselves vulnerable to attacks from lobbies in the anti-Islamic context. The problems of the Muslim community remain. Muslims have not consolidated their communitry into an *Ummah*, and this can only result in weakening their unity. Countries in the British colonial empire were run on a divide-and-rule policy, and the Muslim community in Britain would be naive to think that such efforts will not be made by the British establishment.

The future of Muslim organizations lies in solidarity and unity of purpose, and not divided loyalties to divided masters.

Organizations reflect the nature of the community and the news ones emerging are the 'federations' and 'councils'. Their co-operation is on the basis of common issues facing them. Their unity is fragile, but they have realized their present inability to cope with the problems arising out of interaction with the British context.

The effectiveness of these organizations will be measured in how they resolve the problems of the Muslim community; how they build bridges of understanding with the authorities and how they impart Islamic education.

The most important role they can play is in encouraging the development of Islamic intellectuals. The term intellectuals here is not used in a secular sense. Just like in medieval times the Muslims would produce many Islamic thinkers, there is a need for this today. This need is not only in the Muslim world but also from Britain and other European countries where there are substantial Muslim populations. When the Arabs were in Spain the most famous Arab thinker was Abul Walid Muhammad ibn Ahmed ibn Rushd (1126–1198) of Cordova. He is known in Europe as Averroes and his thought influenced many Christian and Jewish scholars. Whether Muslims may agree with his thought is immaterial. His status as a thinker is acknowledged and undiminished.

Among the intellectuals in the West one has academics who under the influence of Orientalism or other petro-dollar ideologies churn out third rate studies. It is hoped that the younger generation will aspire to become the future thinkers of the Muslims living in the West.

Chapter 9 Youth and Westernization

The greatest fear which haunts the Muslim community is that the younger generation will become westernized, and will lose not only their cultural heritage but also their religion. The fear is real, for Muslim youth is becoming westernized and secularized. In a patriarchal culture like Islam the boys are given more freedom by their parents than the girls. The boys' behaviour is not considered related to the *izzat* (honour) of the Muslim community and whether or not they date English girls, attend *bangra* dances, drink and wear fashionable clothes.

The westernization of Muslim youth takes place through a number of ways. First, the most unobtrusive way in which westernization may take place is through the income factor. When Muslims start work, their income slots them into the class structure of British society. Their income limits their buying power. So if they work in a factory they can only live in inner cities where ghetto housing is cheap. If they are in the professions or business their higher income means they can afford better housing. Income can therefore affect buying power not only with the example of property given above but in all other types of material goods. The danger, however, does not lie here. It comes when the incumbent starts identifying with the class consciousness which may exist within the class they belong to. As a general rule each class has its own class consciousness. Working class thinking differs from the middle and upper classes. Through such class consciousness the youth may get their class ideologies, status symbolism and attitudes of social mixing, buying status symbols, etc. Through class consciousness the youth are sucked into the process of Westernization. Muslim youth has become vulnerable in this way.

Second, the secular education system is another process. Learning about a profession or vocation is one thing but imbibing secular ideologies is another. These penetrate the Muslim mind. Muslims come to believe in 'science' as the only truth if the teacher denigrates 'religions'. Science then becomes the only source of knowledge. As a result of the British educational system young Muslims may know more about the history of the monarchy in Britain than about Islamic history. They are initiated more into the literary culture of Britain than Islam.

The fact is that British culture is not geared towards immigrant children but is directed towards the children of the indigenous population who form the core culture of Britain. So those who think that they have roots in British culture are suffering from 'self-delusions' for 'they are in reality not free but products of a particular culture'.[1] The more they are socialized into British culture the more vulnerable they become to its norms.

Third, westernization takes place through peer group pressure. If this leads Muslim males to imitate the practices approved by the peer group, it can affect their dress, style of speaking, hairstyles, etc. But it can also influence their attitudes towards various activities. The group may date girls and be promiscuous, and the Muslims may follow suit. They may smoke, sniff glue, be on drugs, be gay — all these can be taken from a peer group. This can change the value from Islamic to secular. Some youths have become vulnerable through such pressure.

Fourth, language itself becomes the channel. Speaking in English gives youths access to all the literature written in that language. It becomes a vehicle of communication for the transmission of ideas, values, knowledge and norms, customs, etc. of the dominant society and culture.

Last, the society at large, in which they live, itself becomes an influencing factor through the media, cultural customs, songs, state propaganda, etc. The dominating culture through its ethnocentricism, projection of history, denigration of other cultures, etc. creates low self-images. Those prone to its influences are usually ones who have no self-identity and knowledge of their own past.

The Impact on Muslim Youth

Becoming westernized then is a very easy process for Muslim youth. The crunch comes when in spite of their westernization they are not accepted by British culture, for according to one observer 'the sad truth is that almost all of them are convinced that even if they wanted to feel loyalty to Britain, they would not be allowed to do so by the British'.[2] They are not wrong, for such cultural rejection emanates from the fact that British culture identifies with European culture and not with non-European cultures. The history, culture, language, traditions and customs are different, and however much an individual may become westernized, it remains a thin veneer.

Although such youths can pass their lives on a westernized level, he or she will develop a sense of alienation for he or she knows that British culture accepts neither him nor her. Yet they follow it and its values for they are alienated from their own cultures. They try to become as Westernized as possible in order to be accepted. Its impact creates a generation gap where the youth cannot relate to their parental values. Some feel ashamed of them; others will not even think of keeping them in their homes when they are old. The impact of such alienated youth is very painful for the parents.

The generation gap can cause much tension and conflict in Muslim families. Dr Salim al-Hassani considers that it exerts 'dangerous pressure...from opposing forces: the family demands on the one hand and the alluding attractions of friends on the other. Whilst the lingual and intellectual gap increases between the youth and their parents, the force of attraction into socialising, discos, dance hall, drink parties, mixed camps, sports clubs, girl or boy friends, and its consequent premarital sex, exposure to alcohol, smoking and eventual delinquency also increases'.[3] Such a condition wrecks families from within, leading some parents to say that maybe they made a mistake in emigrating to Britain.

One of the factors which creates generation and cultural gaps is when such sons get married to English girls. They bring another culture into the homes, and direct cultural clashes take place. Such wives often make no attempt to understand the culture, religion or heritage of their husbands. Instead they demean all these aspects of the husband's cultural heritage. The husband in the end hardly has any friends from his own culture. The household has no moral code and the children growing up without any set of Islamic values. Most such marriages are not happy ones and children grow up in a house where there is constant bickering. Constant adjustments need to be made in order to learn the culture of others.

Another cause of alienation is unique. There may be no sence of belonging to mainstream culture but a fascination with it. Such youths may be demeaning their own culture because they suffer from a low self-image. It may be rooted there by the parents who may be westernized or admire western culture. It may be from early schooling in Britain or it may have arisen because the children do not know any other culture for they may not have visited their countries of origin. In short, there can be many reasons but the impact of causing a low self-image means that a young person is lost to the community. Youths who suffer from such low self-images often marry British girls. The blame for such folly cannot just be laid on the youth; it also lies with the parents. The older generation has failed to address the problem and force 'arranged' marriages on their sons and daughters which are rejected. Parents try to arrange marriages on the basis of *biraderi* linkage or sectarian basis. No mechanism has been created where the sexes can meet and select their partners. The 'arranged' marriage is not going to work as more and more youths reject it.

The other impact is alienation from mainstream British culture where the youth wants to belong to his or her own culture but is disillusioned by it in many ways. Some of the responses of Muslim youth reflect this:

"I feel the Muslim youth are showing the tendency to come towards Islam, but with no leadership, the youth is lost. The deviation is more from ourselves than from outside".

"The teachers of Islam do not know how to approach the youth. To the youth they appear strict and backward. Plus the people, who have tried to educate me about Islam only tell me that I must pray five times a day. I already know that. What I would be more interested in knowing is a wider knowledge of Islam".

"Sexual allurements from modern society lures the youth from the values of his own culture.

"The causes are very simple and easy to pick and that is that we have not understood Islam clearly therefore we don't teach our children the true Islam, and a s such, we get a negative result".

"There have been many criticisms by the British public and the media on the Muslim people (youth), especially of Asian origin, not mixing with the rest of the British people and the British ways of life. It is sad that some Muslim youth take into adopting to the system in order to be fully accepted and therefore get absorbed into the society. But what the youth do not know is that the system is not a perfect system and does not conform with Islamic belief. As such they should try to copy only what conforms with their religion and reject what does not conform".

"Two factors are operating in many cases; the parents themselves are not very strongly committed to Islam; secondly, the youth find it difficult to resist the hedonistic attraction all around them – which works through pressure groups".[4]

These responses attribute a wide range of causes of discontent among the Muslim youth ranging from lack of leadership, ignorance of Imams, hedonistic allurements, misunderstanding of Islam, pressure from the dominant society, peer group pressure to lack of commitment of parents. The impact is that the youth became directionless. They walk on a tight rope by being half Westernized and half Easternized.

The third impact goes in favour of Muslims but they have not been able to utilize or exploit the opportunity presented to them. When mainstream culture rejects them racially on the basis of the colour of their skin, the youth often reverts to Islam. As Dr Zaki Badawi points out, 'this ingrained racism is our lifeline — it brings many of our people back to Islam. That's when they start to identify more closely with Islam — some even go to the extent of becoming fundamentalists'.[5] This creates the basis for reactionary Islam. As stated above the Muslim community has failed to channel this reaction. The Muslim community has not produced any blueprints or models. As al-Hassani also observes, 'the Muslim community in Britain is far from being able to pose as an example to be followed'.[6] We have stated that the community is confused because their Islam is reactionary. The youth will therefore be further confused in following Islam for as al-Hassani points out: 'The dilemma of Muslims will continue on how to live their lives under the present British law without violating some of their religious beliefs and practices. The danger, however, is that a state of affairs might emerge where the Muslims will tend to adopt a character which some people accuse the Jews of having. That is the type of psycho with a two-sided behaviour, one with the clan and the other with the Gentiles. The faith of a Muslim, however, cannot accommodate such a practice'.[7]

The Muslim community has failed the younger generation because they themselves hold reactionary and obscurantist views of Islam. Specifically the community has failed to create an attractive Islamic environment or make mosques into community centres where the younger generation can meet other Muslims socially. They have not been able to define Islamic values and standards in a clear-cut manner. Regarding the youth problem they have not been able to suggest alternative Islamic ways. Instead patriarchal hypocrisy prevails: boys are allowed to do what they want. The youth may seduce English girls for premarital sex but not Muslim girls. In Birmingham a slight variation of this case has been observed where Pakistani young men did not want to date English but Asian girls so they targeted Sikh girls. This led to Sikh gangs (Sher-e-Punjab) and Pakistani gangs (Black Panthers) engaging in street fights. The fact is that premarital sex is immoral in Islam and such permutations do not absolve the Muslims. While this example focuses only on the sexual aspect, there are many other areas where there is an escape from reality and a lapse into obscurantism which have left the youth who have reverted to Islam confused. Needless to say such confusion arises when the parents have not been able to set an example themselves of a practising Islamic family. Parents have not developed open communication with their children and won their trust and confidence. Furthermore the parents have not been able to define the relationship of the child to their own community and mainstream culture. The youth have not been pushed into Islamic work, for the community, as already stated, has not created such avenues. This failure of the Muslim community has taken its toll on its youth.

Conclusion

The challenges facing the Muslim youth are very serious. They are the hope of the future but have no models to follow from the past or present. They are forced to evolve their own Islamic identities as best as they can from existing resources which may be limited or non existent. But every path is full of controversies and contradictions.

The Muslim youth therefore have to develop a strong Islamic identity which does not emanate from reaction and is based on a sound understanding of Islam. If the Muslim community does not facilitate this for the youth, then they will have lost the future generation. If they repeat the same mistakes of the past generations, then the community will remain static. The understanding of Islam has to transcend the sectarian, class, ethnic and cultural barriers in which they are imprisoned. Not until the youth get into *taruf* (getting to know one another), *Nush* (exchanging advice for understanding) and *Takaful* (mutual support from each other) can a collective Islamic identity for Muslim youth develop.

In order to facilitate this a number of steps have to be taken:
1. Holding summer camps where parents can send their young sons and daughters so that not only a correct understanding of Islam is given but also a correct way of behaving between the two sexes is put into practice on the basis of the three concepts given above. The inculcation of love and practice of the faith as well as discipline has to be developed through such exercises. This should be under the supervision of experienced Islamic youth leaders and Imams who are above sectarianism.

2. Muslim youth should hold meetings and seminars where any issue is thrashed out frankly on an Islamic basis.
3. Community centres have to be established in mosques where the youth can play, meet, learn and discuss and become aware of the problems of the community as well as learn about Islam through Islamic education.
4. English-speaking Imams have to take over mosques.
5. Islamic youth counsellors should be working in every mosque.
6. All Muslim youth should learn Arabic fluently as their language of conversation irrespective of whether they speak Arabic or are non-Arabs. Their own cultural languages should be secondary. English should be their first language so that they will interact with the mainstream culture. But in order to counteract the influences of mainstream culture they must be able to understand the Qur'an directly through Arabic. Their own cultural languages cannot teach them Islam and can only teach them their ethnic culture — not Islamic culture.
7. Learning Arabic will also help the youth to form study circles in which they can discuss and argue about the meaning of the Qur'an and evaluate the old *tafsirs* (interpretations). The fact is that with the Qur'an no *tafsir* can be final but only relative relating to the time and era of the writers.

Chapter 10 *Muslim Women and Freedom*

The problem of Muslim women is a serious one for the Muslim community. It is compounded by the reactionary Islam of the Muslim community in Western society which is very sensitive about Muslim women. The problem however is not the Muslim women. On the contrary, they are the victims. The problem emanates from the community. A random sample conducted on Muslim women yielded frank replies on a number of issues which will give an idea of the discontent among Muslim women of their lot. 'The Muslim community does not care about other Muslims. If a woman does need help she goes to a white person, for they are seen as more helpful and understanding'. 'The joint families that are in our community are always the main problem'. 'Husbands don't treat women right. They treat them like dirt'. 'The continuous condemnation of the female role by the community in the name of Islam. They are totally misinformed by the Mullahs'. 'Too much segregation between groups of Muslims in gatherings. There should be full co-operation between them as Muslim brothers and sisters'. 'They gave my brother a chance to go into higher education whereas me and my sisters have no say. The community misinterprets Islam according to their needs'.[1]

Most of these responses show a reaction to the attitudes of parents. One respondent pointed to the crux of the problem suffered by Muslim women: 'Young Muslim women simply have no freedom whatsoever, they have less freedom than male Muslims half their age. No doubt parents and elders may ask freedom to do what? Well, in a word, freedom to be a human not an excuse for one, living under restrictions as if her entire teenage life were a forbidden age with which she needs help to overcome'.[2] This problem is serious for it shows

84

not only a basic distrust of women, but in British society, which places a high premium on individual freedom, such oppression can only turn them against the faith. The tragedy is that the structures of such tyranny as considered by the above respondent are considered to be 'the view of the Muslim community' and related to the 'parents *izzat*'. A clear-cut distinction which should be made here again is that the attitudes and behaviour of the Muslim community is not a reflection of Islam but of the patriarchal society they come from. If it was Islamic then their societies should have been Islamic and their countries Islamic states. Instead the Muslim communities' attitudes and behaviour emanate mainly from patriarchal norms embedded in the historical context peculiar to their countries of origin. For example, the Sudanese custom of circumcising their women reflects the custom of Sudanese society and the custom of the Pakistani 'arranged' marriage reflects the custom prevalent in the Pakistani society

The norms of the patriarchal culture from where they came determines the view of Muslim women, which conflicts with the British culture. First, women are considered to be a liability as they will leave the house when they get married, while males are considered to be assets. Male children are given more importance since they will not only carry the inheritance and family name but they are also capital investment for economic reasons. This norm emanates from the patriarchal structure of village societies and conflicts with British culture where the view is that both sexes are considered equally important and independent. This custom also conflicts with the Islamic norm which expects no discrimination between the sexes.

Second, there follows from the above another norm — that education is not necessary for women, for they may become 'too clever' for the men. There is no preference for wives who are too highly qualified. This again conflicts with the British education system where every child has to receive education until the age of 16. Often after 16 Muslim girls are withdrawn from school and not allowed any further education in British society. This custom also conflicts with the Islamic norm which does not restrict Muslim women from having education.

Third, the role of women is restricted to cooking for their husbands and bearing children. Such a role definition effectively puts a full stop to any career aspirations girls may have. This again conflicts with the norms of British culture where girls are free to choose any career. It also conflicts with the Islamic norm which does not restrict women from working to support themselves or their families.

Fourth, there is a basic distrust of womanhood and its sexuality. This emanates from the view that a woman is considered as 'property' rather than as a person. Property must be safeguarded for if it is 'damaged' through sexual contact it can bring 'dishonour' and 'shame' on the family. According to this concept, 'the woman in a family, through proper behaviour brings honour to the men of the family so that their honour and prestige (and secondarily that of the women) are maintained, if not enhanced. For this reason, if she transgresses it, it is she who is punished by the family rather than the man. Although according to the Qur'an and the teaching of the Prophet, God requires the same standard of moral conduct from both sexes, in practice the picture is very different'.[3] Men can be sexually promiscuous and are not supposed to have defiled the *Izzat* of the family. But such behaviour also breaks the Islamic norm.

Slander is also forbidden by Islam but in practice it is prevalent and focuses on women. A Pakistani woman had to challenge her husband's assertion, in the British court, when he accused her from the very first night of her marriage that she was 'not good' and had had sex with other men. He did not consummate the arranged marriage and the case was heard under the 1891 Slander of Women Act. The woman was found to be a virgin, and the judge when awarding her damages of £20,000 stated that in the Pakistani community such an accusation is considered a 'grave insult'[4] against a woman. The patriarchal cultural norms rather than the Islamic ones still prevail in the Muslim community. Such obsession with having 'virgin' brides led to the importing of brides from Pakistan. Sometime ago the Home Office, suspecting that its immigration laws were being abused, had the diabolical idea of conducting 'virginity tests' on imported virgins to see whether or not they were virgo intacta. The idea was abandoned when it was exposed.

Fifth, a girl must be obedient and subservient to the wishes of the family. Any expression of self-opinions are considered to threaten the power of the patriarchal household. This again conflicts with the norms of British society where individualism is considered to be a prime quality to be found in a person. It is a conflict with the Islamic norm where a Muslim woman is expected to stand up for her rights and forbid any un-Islamic action.

The various responses show that there is a serious conflict between parental patriarchal and Islamic norms. Such a problem starts early as socialization at home and at schools presents two different models. According to Sharif, 'most of the difficulties these girls experience arise from out of the emotional conflict which develops between the contrasting socialization by parents and the socialization in the school. This creates varying degrees of anxiety and ambivalence about their self-images. The girls who are in direct conflict with their parents are also the ones who are marginally more involved with British culture and consequently are more animated but paradoxically are more in danger of becoming alienated'.[5] Such conflicts are bound to increase among Muslim women. Compulsory education until the age of 16 must influence them at this impressionable age. If the parents are only able to come up with patriarchal answers and the girls mistakenly regard that as Islam, they are bound to rebel against Islam.

In order to impose patriarchal norms, it is not surprising to find that men resort to extremes such as observed by the researcher that 'I was informed by some of the women that many Pakistani girls have been removed from school because parents fear that their *Izzat* at stake. Some girls are paying high price for bringing dishonour to the family. Some are incarcerated (locked in their bedrooms, confined to the house), beaten, forcibly married, either in Britain or in Pakistan'.[6] The concept of *Izzat,* the male domination and female submission syndrome, the female sexual distrust syndrome, the female as property — all are so deep rooted in the Muslim's patriarchal culture. The ownership of women is so strong that a father cut the throat of his daughter when she wanted to become a Christian.[7]

In other cases Muslim girls have developed a phobia at such behaviour and considered it better to marry English husbands.[8] In another case, a newly married bride hanged herself because she found herself incompatible with her 'arranged' bridegroom from Pakistan. Among Asian girls the Muslim girl stands out to researchers for, as one observer comments, they 'are expected to be deferential to their parents' authority and after puberty Muslim girls are 'closely guarded'.[9] Guarding women in a culture which grants its women freedom reflects a distrust originating from their countries of origin. It is almost similar to the phobia of medieval England when crusaders used 'chastity belts' on their women to preserve their virtue.

The chastity-belt syndrome of the Muslim community towards its women opens two choices to the latter: a life of imprisonment versus a life of freedom. Faced with such choices the Muslim community may soon find that its girls are more easily assimilated into Western culture than the males. The fault will not be of the secular culture but of the Muslim community itself if they do not know how to handle the younger generation of women.

How can Muslims expect their girls to remain with Islam when no Islamic education has been imparted to them? The state of Islamic education has already been described but the education of girls is even more ignored. There are few, if any, qualified Muslim female teachers in Islam. Knowing how to read and recite the Qur'an does not qualify a person to teach it and there are 'qualified' male teachers, but the parents are reluctant to send their daughters to them or to 'mixed' schools. The most crucial period of education is during the period of puberty and early adolescence when the girls are maturing and are more vulnerable to influences from their peer groups, Western culture, television, books, magazines, etc. Parents may tell their daughters to leave the room when sexual scenes are being shown on television, but can they watch over the shoulders of their daughters 24 hours a day? What, as is often the case, if the girls are intelligent and undergo professional training for various degrees? Will parents send them to universities in other cities to study in educational institutions and stay in dormitories where there is bound to be interaction between the sexes? A number of points therefore need serious thinking by the Muslim communities.

First, if the Muslim women are not educated the future of the Muslim community is doomed. Every Muslim woman has to have vocational or professional training. Not only is this essential to the economic survival and upward mobility of families, but in the highly industrialized societies non-educated persons remain at the bottom of it. With illiterate mothers the future generations of Muslim children will suffer.

Second, the Muslim community has to sort out its thinking on another issue: whether Muslim women have to have an Islamic identity or not, or is it only the males who are entitled to Islam? Looking at the mosques one would think that only males were required to pray, for women are not allowed in mosques. Some Muslims have realized this fact and have made provision for prayers to be offered by women in their mosques. But most of them have no such provision. So how are Muslim women going to develop Islamic identities? The home and the mosques have to play an important role, which they have so far not done. The home has to be a place where Islamic values have to be taught and the mosques where the social culture of Islam has to be practised. No amount of Islamic education which does not inculcate Islamic values from the home and which is realizable in the mosque as the community centre will ever take root. The home, the mosque, the Muslim community are the media through which Islamic education can be inculcated in Muslim women.

But the test of all this training and teaching lies in the public areas of life in Western society and not in the home or the mosque. No Muslim girl can be kept locked away. They have to be sent to school and further education may see them at university. If they have internalized the values of Islam, they will know how to conduct themselves in the public areas where both males and females interact. But the Muslim community does not seem to have any faith in its girls or that the teachings of Islam could be absorbed by them. They have not understood the fact that in the secular Western society it is the individual's 'no' and not community pressure which will matter. Any girl can go to her doctor and take the contraceptive pill, and the doctor cannot disclose it to her parents — nor do the parents have any rights to demand it of the doctor. It is only the girl who decides whether she wants it or not.

The test of any moral teaching rests on the individual responsibility determined by the Islamic moral code internalized by Muslims. The problems pointed to are 'it seems that isolation and lack of knowledge are two of the main problems faced by Muslim women in Britain'.[10] The solution to these is to come out of isolation and confront ignorance at every step of one's life. If the Muslim women do not have knowledge about Islam, they will not be able to distinguish patriarchal customs from Islamic culture. This can only be done if they follow the Qur'an and the *Sunnah* as primary and secondary sources, and think about them and not blindly follow any interpretations about Islam. Khalida Khan is right when she observes that 'the Western idea of the position of women in Islam is well known and the teachers are also influenced by their own prejudices and ignorance of Islam. Because the Muslim girls are not receiving positive images of Islam, they begin to lose self-esteem, confidence and pride...she has no value'.[11] It is not surprising then to find out why Muslim girls suffer from a low self-image. Others get out of the pail of Islam and make a place for themselves in the secular culture. They consider religion to be 'something that was created donkeys years ago to keep the masses quiet and give something to people to believe in'.[12] Others, on the other hand, did not have sex with boyfriends but dated boys and 'a little modest dalliance was not ruled out'.[13] Still others, seeing no option, ran away from oppressive parents and took refuge in the various refuge homes for Asian women.

The problem of the transmission of Islamic values is a serious one. Tasneem Afzal explains the issue very well when she writes: 'We can be taught the Islamic way of life by our elders and by our religious leaders, but we cannot be taught to grasp a truth with our soul. We cannot be "taught" a personal closeness in our hearts with our Creator. Any form of teaching can be helped towards "religion" in this spirtual sense by encouragement to search inside themselves to find the vacuum that needs truth, stability and love. Then the person must discover for themselves a sense or perception of the Almighty and surrendering one's soul. The problem for for many young Muslim people today is that Islam is misrepresented as a package of rules, a bundle of do's and don'ts'.[14] A very subtle point has been raised here that depth of belief can only be created by personal experience of Islam. This can only be done if Islam is not presented as a 'package of rules' but through the presentation of its essence which has to be absorbed. Such an essence can only be understood if there is a conceptual understanding of Islam.

Another girl expresses how such understanding can be developed: 'Generally speaking Muslim women may well deviate from Islam. Outward appearances such as the type of dress she wears (or the way in which she covers her body) and the manner in which she conducts herself are easily apparent. However, it is what lies under the surface — that I think is very important — in the way she perceives Islam. Her way of thinking (does she think it just a set of rules and regulations laid down by parents?) Unfortunately, I do fear that so many Muslim women have overlooked the true beauty of Islam. They don't realise what a privilege it is to be born a Muslim. They probably know the pillers of Islam but they don't understand the reason behind it and therefore may not grasp its meaning'.[15] Here again an important point has to be understood. If Islamic rules are imposed on Muslims, they can easily throw them off in a secular culture. But if the rules grow inside them, those rules will express themselves through the Muslims and start making an impact on the secular culture.

But any attempt to impose the patriarchal value system on Islam will not be accepted. For instance, considerations of *biraderi* and class often prompt parents to import bridegrooms for arranged marriages for their daughters. But according to Nasreen Din, 'the problem arises when the girls right to give consent is ignored. The other side of the coin is where a Muslim girl and boy meet independently and wish to marry. Matters like boys' parents' occupational background and the girls' parents' traditional class status should be squashed and paramountcy given to the suitability of both the girl and the boy'.[16] Arranged marriages where the girls right to consent has not been obtained are un-Islamic. While in Pakistan such consent may be forcibly extorted through threats, it is not possible in Britain. It has to be negotiated.

Many such problems confronting Muslim women cannot be discussed due to lack of space. But the dilemma facing the Muslim community is serious. If steps are not taken to give consideration to the points raised, the social distance and estrangement of Muslim women from the community will increase. The reason for this has been well put by Raana Bhatti: 'The struggle to be a Muslim has become largely if not indeed totally an individual and personal one. When Muslims attempt to live as a community, unfortunately, certain very negative facets came to the forefront of every action, i.e. hypocrisy, deceit and dishonesty. In addition any attempt at communal activity seems to bring a type of religious "blackmail" into effect. By this I mean that certain prominent members of a group tend to force individuals to conform to a particular interpretation of Islam. This leads to a particular interpretation of Islam. This leads to an environment within the community in which there is lack of tolerance, lack of tolerance, lack of humility, lack of real choice and exploitation of the many by the few. The whole attempt at a communal lifestyle therefore becomes some kind of a staged affair where each Muslim tries with his neighbour to win a personal award as "Best Muslim of the Year". To my mind, an obvious question arises: who are the Muslims practising Islam for? – themselves? In which case they are on the biggest ego trip of their lives. – or is it for Allah and themselves? In which case it would be *shirk*. Or is it for Allah alone? If it was for the latter than Muslims would be examples for mankind instead of what they actually are – objects of contempt, ridicule and ever increasing hatred'.[17]

There are a number of 'best Muslims' of the year to be found in the community who seek platforms in order to articulate their views of Islam. For example, one Muslim on the matter of girls acquiring a career pontificated: 'We would prefer them to lose out in the world rather than lose out in the Hereafter'.[18] Such a view shows an utter lack of the understanding of Islam for the Qur'an is a book of action prescribed for this world, not the Hereafter. It is here that the Islamic state, society and civilization can be created, not in the Hereafter. Any actions in this world are to be judged in the *Akhirah* (Hereafter) so no Muslim can afford to lose out in this world.

In fact Muslim women in Britain have begun to take action in this world, as one Western news reporter discovered when she went asking questions of some Muslim women. She observed that 'they say that Islam has provided them with the self-confidence to assert themselves as women'.[19] One of the women interviewed, Dr Sheila Qureshi, said: 'I am breaking new ground as a woman chemist already. Can I really be expected to pioneer as both a woman and a Muslim?'[20] This shows how the development of a Muslim self-identity can express itself. The struggle that Muslim women face in

94

evolving their own Muslim self-identity cannot be underrated, for as Farida Hussain points out 'the interpretation of Islam by women has yet to emerge in the Muslim world. But where it has been done, it has led to role conflicts because the personal role definitions by women are incompatible with the role expectations of the Muslim males. Such role conflicts have often arisen as a reaction to the retrogressive Islamic forces and have led to women adopting alien ideologies such as feminism. Other Muslims have reacted to Western modernization and have adopted Marxist ideologies. Both these options chosen by Muslim women have failed to become grounded in the context due to the fact that they are reactionary manifestations. Undoubtedly, such courses of action have been chosen in desperation by Muslim women but they have not resulted in solving the problems of Muslim women. Changes in the role performance must evolve from within the Islamic role structure through personal role definitions evolved by Muslim women. In other words, social change in the role of Muslim women must be brought about by the elimination of feudal Islam through Islam. Such processes as stated earlier must start by evaluation of all interpretations and re-examining the Qur'an and the *Hadith* for oneself. Although a cut and dried solution may not be readily available because of the opposition from the retrogressive forces, but in it lies the salvation for Muslim women'.[21] Muslim women must therefore read the Qur'an and contemplate its message seriously.

Conclusion

The Muslim community will have to redefine its role behaviour of Muslim women. Hitherto role behavioural definitions have been from the patriarchal point of view passed off as Islamic. Such patriarchal interpretations have tremendous power in the villages of the country of origin of

Muslims where a communal pressure is applied for conformity. In Britain such communal pressures are not powerful as any girl who runs away from home can find accommodation in homes for runaway females.

The Muslim community has to realize that commitment to Islam is personal and not communal. Families have to invest in cultivating personal commitments and not leave it to the *biraderi* which is run by patriarchal rules. The depth of faith of every individual is personal, for in Islam each one is held personally responsible for their actions and no one else can take on someone else's responsibility.

The personal commitment acts as a form of social control from within. The Islamic identity acts as a form of personal control. The stronger the Islamic identity the stronger the inner control which will be exercised. The communal identity in which a person can bring dishonour to the *izzat* of the parents does not work on the secular culture. Parents therefore have to recognize this characteristic of secular cultures, otherwise they can soon find themselves bereft of their girls.

Chapter 11　*New Muslims Between Cultures*

Historically, Islam entered into many European countries a long time ago and has stayed there right into the 20th century. The fact that Islam is found in many East European countries is because the Ottoman Turks had converted the indigenous population to Islam. Before the Turks, the Arabs in Spain had converted the Spanish to Islam. But once Spain fell into Spanish hands, various types of coercion by the Inquisition authorities who were full of hatred and hostility to Islam forced the converts back to Christianity. Even today, hatred and hostility manifests itself in Bulgaria where anti-Islamic groups are forcing native Muslim citizens to change their religion and names to Bulgarian. Thousands of Bulgarians have fled to Turkey. In other cases, Yugoslavian Islamic thinkers like Alija Ali Izetbegovic have suffered imprisonment for writing books on Islam.[1] Such ruthless steps have not as yet been taken against English converts to Islam. At one point England came very near conversion to Islam as King John (1199–1216) sent a delegation to the Ahmohad Moroccan king to give him military aid in return for his embracing Islam. The request was turned down by the ruler. But over the centuries, even after the Crusades, British interests remained in the Muslim world. An Englishman, William Henry Quilliam became a Muslim after a visit to Morocco and started a small Islamic movement back in his native Liverpool. Soon afterwards another English convert, Marmaduke Pickthall, emerged and his today there are many new Muslims in Britain.

The contributions of converts like Pickthall should not be underrated. Marmaduke Pickthall was an English Tory and vehemently opposed British schemes and war against the Ottoma Empire, which estranged him from his fellow countrymen. He also worked in the service of the Nizam of

Hyderabad in India and under the Nizam's patronage and produced one of the finest translation of the Qur'an in English, entitled *'The Meaning of the Glorious Qur'an*. He delivered a series of lectures on Madras in 1925 which was published under the title *'The Cultural Side of Islam'*. Pickthall did his best to help Muslims in the Middle East, India and England. In London he formed an Islamic information bureau and published a journal entitled *Muslim Outlook*. But he is known among Muslims for his translation and forgotten for his other services.[2]

Some converts made attempts to start their own Islamic centres. One such Muslim was Shaikh Abd al-Qadir al-Sufi who aimed to start a Sufi *Zawiya* in Britain. Becoming a disciple of a Sufi Shaykh of the Darqawiyya Sufi Tariqa, he gathered a large following all over the world and in 1976 decided to settle in Norwich and form a 'Muslim village' of believers in the U.K. His first book, *The Way of Muhammad,* (published in 1975), was in this vein. But his thinking by the late 1970s had changed to activism and anti-nationalism. His book, *Jihad – A Ground Plan* (published in 1978), reflected his activist Islamic stance. In the meantime a number of problems started emerging in the community in the 'retreat-cum-military garrison from which the Murabitun (singular Murabit) emerged'.[3] He also began advocating strongly the Maliki school of law. Due to his dogmatic and autocratic attitude the community soon began disintegrating. Abd al-Qadir had a small following in Granada (Spain) and he made a *hijra* (emigration) there to establish a *ribat* (garrison retreat). The *Murabitun* in Norwich today are a well organised community and are conceptually clear about their Islamic views and contains number of Islamic scholars.

Indigenous Muslims have formed an organization called the British Muslim Association, which is located in London. Some Muslims like Yusuf Islam are actively engaged in helping the Muslim community. He opened the Islamia

Primary School in London and it has been very successfully adminsitering educational services to the community. Many new Muslims including well-known names such as Sarah Malik, Maryam Davies, Ruqayah Khalil, Meryl Wyn Davies, Ahmad Thompson and Abdul Hakim Winter have contributed by writing books on Islam. Muslim women are actively engaged in giving speeches on Islam all over the country. Some converts have even launched in Britain an Islamic Party as mentioned earlier.

Although Britain offers good scope for conversions *(Dawah)* the fact still remains that the Muslim community has not taken advantage of it. Members of the indigenous population who have become Muslims have embraced Islam largely due to their own efforts of finding Islam as the best answer to their problems. There have been many complaints against the Saudi funded Islamic Mission and others that they have not made any effort to do so. One complaint from an English convert was that Muslims conduct their meetings in Urdu which the indigenous people cannot understand. Most of them are incapable of speaking in proper English and, as such, cannot explain Islam to the non-Muslim. In general no enthusiastic efforts are made or imaginative techniques employed to attract non-Muslims to Islam. Due to lack of research Muslims do not even know why non-Muslims embrace Islam. The only substantial and original piece of research was done by Mrs Harfiyah Ball-Haleem, who did a survey on new Muslim women.[4] The Western women who embraced Islam found that the Western society in which they lived had 'no sense of direction' and that their lives seemed 'unsettled', 'pointless and empty' without any 'guidance' or 'certainty'. Some felt that in their personal lives they 'had no feeling of purpose' or that they had 'no religion', 'no code of behaviour to help...in difficulties' or that they were 'limited to the aims of this life'. The most significant finding of this study was that the majority of the British women converts had embraced Islam through personal contact with Muslims who projected Islamic behaviour. It was not done through handing them a copy of the Qur'an. Once having embraced Islam some converts also gave insights into what they felt. In human relationships the women felt 'closeness, love, kindness, caring', 'feeling of belonging to a family', 'feeling of oneness and common humanity' and 'confidence in dealing with people', 'made me feel the need to discipline my life in a positive way'. These women were all very lucky in finding out what they had sought through Islam. The Muslim community in general has made no effort to accommodate them.

The divisive factor here is culture and ideologies. If they are converted by Arabs the convert may become 'Arabized' or, if by a Pakistani, the convert may become Pakistanized'. Without that they are not considered to be 'proper' Muslims.

It is also a fact that Muslim converts have to suffer most because of the anti-Islamic structure of British society. In some cases, girls who have embraced Islam have been turned out of their homes by their parents. Others have suffered racism in reverse. According to one respondent: 'The last 11 years of my life since I have converted to Islam have not been good. I was married...an experience which if accurately described, was hell. An even more traumatic divorce followed. In many ways being a Muslim helped, but in many ways it did not. My biggest problem was I found I was discriminated against because I was an English Muslim. Born Muslims are so warm and hospitable to converts; they have endless patience and energy when dealing with Islamic problems, i.e. how to fast, how to pray, etc. But when faced with real life problems they do not want to know. After six months of trying to seek advice about my problems, during which time I spoke with six different authorities on Islam from various mosques, I was finally told, "You are English, go to your own law, we cannot help you". In the end Islam was used against me, because of my lack of knowledge and because I was an English convert'.[5] This letter shows the attitude of the Muslim community and their total failure in providing new Muslims with a home which is more warmer than their own homeland.

The attitude towards women converts is particularly appalling. Another Muslim woman convert explains the point clearly: 'I am in disagreement with those members of the Ummah and the Ulama who refuse to recognise the fact that women can and do contribute greatly to Islam. Innumerable times that I have quoted *Surah XXXIII: 35* and *Surah XIII: 97* to sisters and brothers who think that women are not equal to men, and that they should be snuggly shut away and not permitted to lead active and useful lives. Please do not think that I do not see a wife and mother's place as being a very special one in Islam. But I believe that we Muslimahs must be active as well, and by "active" I mean leading lives that are not restrained and limited by tradition and ritualisation...What I think we are dealing with here is not just male chauvinism but male paranoia as well. I have always been struck by the way in which some Muslims see women in general as being a destructive force, rather than granting them an independent intellectual and spiritual status in the world of Islam'.[6] The point raised of equality between the sexes in Islam is just as important as the reasons for it being attributed to 'male chauvinism' and 'male paranoia'. English women are the worst sufferers for the Muslim community has not made any arrangements for them to be welcomed into the faith.[7]

The new Muslims also face the problems of being between two cultures. Ibrahim Hewitt correctly observed that 'the two-headed syndrome often afflicts new Muslims. We all experience it sometimes – you walk into a mosque and every head turns slowly and blatantly to stare at you, suspicion oozing towards you. After checking your flies, you realise that they are not looking at a fellow Muslim, they are looking at a white man who has intruded on the Asian ghetto'.[8] This is due to the fact that most Muslims have not accepted a universal perspective on Islam in practice and cannot step out of their cultural boundaries to accept Muslims from other cultures. The white image is considered superior to their low self-image. Some Asians have a rude shock when the white women they marry turn to Islam and become more Islamic than they are.

New Muslims enrich the culture of Islam. They may break some of the un-Islamic traditional practices and attitudes prevailing in the Muslim community. One new Muslimah on the issue of 'hijab' retorted: 'I am profoundly bored with men pontificating on what is and is not acceptable hijab. I wear what I like to consider to be hijab that complies with the demands of the Holy Qur'an and, when I am abroad, I wear whatever is acceptable to my sister there. If they wear *el-Ziyy/niqab*, then so do I. But I do not waste my time entering into endless discussions about what degree of modesty is necessary, and most of the sisters of my age do the same. So is it not about time that certain elements in the Ummah and Ulama let us abide by our consciences in the matter of our dress? Or do they want to continue judging all Muslimahs as mindless and irresponsible children?'[9] On another important issue the new Muslimahs observed that 'I have yet to find a member of the Ummah who I felt would make a satisfactory husband. Please do not think that I am holding out for the "ideal" husband – I hope that I am enough of a realist to know that such a man does not exist, or, if he does, the odds of his coming into my life are highly remote. But I have found...that so many Muslims are looking for wives who will spend their time cooking and procreating. I enjoy cooking and I look forward to bearing children but they are not, in my opinion, the be-all and end-all of a women's existence. My ambition is to cook and procreate but also to continue in the best way I can for Islam. Motherhood is a duty that I full accept, but I would like to think that I can also offer something in addition by using the talents that Almighty Allah gave me at birth'.[10] These are serious questions which need to be considered, and new Muslims may help to clear the confusion between traditions, cultures, customs and Islam.

Conclusion

The most important factor which has to be recognized is that, if Islam has to be rooted in British society, it must expand among the indigenous population. The sons of immigrant Muslims may have been born in Britain, but they do not have the same history and will always remain immigrants. But nobody can label the indigenous Muslim community as immigrants or think of sending them to their 'country of origin'.

Both the groups need to work together as well as cement relations through marriage. This has not happened on a significant scale. Most Muslims marry non-Muslim girls and become secularized. They suffer from a low self-image and their efforts to assimilate themselves and their children knows no limits. They have nothing to sustain themselves from within and are ultimately very disappointed when the mainstream culture rejects them.

Another factor which it is important to realize is that in the British culture the Islamic alternative has to be presented in an attractive manner which will not only raise the self-image of Muslims but also offer salvation to Westerners. This has not received any attention because the Muslim community is still engrossed in its petty disputes and does not even project a clear-cut worldview and perspective of Islam. The present face of Islam is sufficient to drive away non-Muslims from Islam. In order to present Islam as a powerful alternative to the dominant tradition and powerful Western civilization, it has to be presented in an equally attractive manner. It has to be a self-sufficient package of a civilization within a civilization which comprises much more than the five pillars of Islam.

103

The Muslims in Britain have had a low self-image for they had neither an Islamic State to look up to in the Middle East nor any significant achievements in the United Kingdom.

In the United Kingdom, they have been under considerable constraints as the four structures racial, secular, anti-Islamic and internal colonialism, did not give them enough space to be themselves. These four structures are briefly discussed below.

The Racial Structure

Much has been written about racism in British society and there is no need to dwell on the subject here. It is sufficient to state that racial discrimination and prejudice based on the colour of people's skin are widespread in society. It affects not only the Muslims but also members of other ethnic minorities such as Hindus, Sikhs and Afro-Caribbeans. On the micro level it may erupt into daily racial violence and abuse in working class neighbourhoods and council estates. In other areas like jobs and institutions it may manifest itself through 'institutionalized racism'.

Racism dates from the time when racism became a formal ideology to legitimize British rule over the colonies through myths of superiority of race or civilization. As the post-World War II economic climate created labour shortages in Britain, the government overcame the problem by importing labour from their former colonies. If Muslims accept racism, then they develop low self-images of themselves as 'inferior'. Some find ways of overcoming it by Anglicizing their names, while others try to assimilate themselves into British culture. When racism poses as an obstacle to their assimilation, then they start thinking of questions related to identities: who am I – British, Pakistani or Muslim? Institutions created by the

104

British like the Commission for Racial Equality have been nothing more than facades.[1]

The Secular Structure

The context of British society is again secularist. While churches have their congregations they are neither full nor have any impact on the political structures of British society. Religion is a personal matter. This is due to the secular ideas which emerged with the industrial revolution. Secularism in so far as it denies the existence of God gives rise to all kinds of philosophies and ideologies of life and is in direct opposition to Islam.

One aspect of such secularism can be labelled as modernism, another as morality. Those with a little knowledge of Islam would not know how to react to its values. Muslims confronted with such a secular context find it difficult to handle the value conflicts challenging their lifestyles, which arise through the situational ethics of British society. Situational ethics change according to the needs of the situation. The Muslim community resident within this society is interacting with it at every level. For example, Muslim children are studying in British schools where sex education teaches them that nothing is wrong with premarital heterosexual behaviour. This conflicts with the Islamic values, for teaching the physiology of sexual anatomy is different from secular sexual values in sex education. Questions like these affecting the daily lives of hundreds of young people still remain controversial.

The Anti-Islamic Structure

The above-mentioned structure may be confronted by other non-Muslim ethnic minorities. But the anti-Islamic structure especially confronts the Muslim because the West has experienced it historically. It is much older than the racist ideology of colonialism and dates back to the early Crusades when England fought against Muslims and lost.

The hostility in Britain from the media and other quarters against Islam erupted over the publication of *The Satanic Verses* by Salman Rushdie, which gave ample proof of how the hatred of Islam is deeply rooted in this structure. It was done in the name of 'freedom of expression' but it provided a good example of the anti-Islamic tradition. The 'British' Muslims know where they stand. The Rushdie affair further added fuel to the hatred of Islam just as much as there was a real fear that in world affairs Islam was becoming the central force.[1] The fear is similar to that voiced by a British MP who was disturbed by the protests of Muslims on the Rushdie affair and said that Britain must be reconquered for the British and 'when Muslims say that they cannot live in a country where Salman Rushdie is free to express his view, they should be told...go back from whence you come'.[2] The fear expressed by the MP is very real for, when the countries in the European Community become a single market in 1992, the four structures being discussed will combine their power to oppress the Muslims.

The Internal Colonialism Structure

The nostalgia about the British Raj is still strong in Britain. Some political elites and some institutions still suffer from the colonial syndrome. They have not 'decolonized' their minds of this idea. The attitude of internal colonialism then refuses to accept the fact that British society has become multicultural. It is still interested in reinforcing the classic colonial theory of Lord Macaulay who formulated his famous minutes on education for British India in 1835 in which it was stated that 'we must at present do our best to form a class who may be interpreters between us and the millions whom we govern: a class of persons, Indian in blood and colour, but English in taste, in opinions, in morals and intellect'.[3] But that class was produced and served British

106

interests in their colonial empire. As British citizens in Britain the immigrant population was not the subject people. This hypocrisy gets exposed when the four structures affect not only the Muslims but also other minority communities of non-Muslim Asians and Afro-Caribbeans. But it must be said that, since Muslims are the largest minority, their historical interaction with the British has singled them out.

Under the four structural constraints, three options are given to Muslims by the assimilationist, isolationist and integrationist lobbies. The assimilationists perspective is reflected in a classic policy statement in which he explained that the 'right relationship' should be to go along with the 'dominant tradition – Western, Christian and Liberal' because no ethnic minority can 'isolate itself from the mainstream of British life'.[4] The assimilationist perspective attempts to create the Lord Macaulay ideal types[5] and fails to see the contradiction with the colonial idealism.

The isolationist perspective is evident in the Muslim Manifesto issued by The Muslim Institute in London.[6] The Muslim Manifesto aims to set up a Council of British Muslims which will act as a 'Muslim Parliament'. There will be other bodies like the General Assembly which will meet once a year and its membership will be by invitation from the Muslim community. In addition, there will be leaders of Muslim youth and Muslim women. The general thrust of the manifesto is that 'the options of integration and/or assimilation as official policy in Britain must be firmly resisted and rejected and the community should develop their own identity and culture within Britain'.[7] How was this view received by other Muslims in Britain? The editorial comment in *The Muslim News* (London) was that it was 'far from assured' that it could work for when with 'institutions being identified as having external influences...consensus is not easily reached'.[8] A prominent Muslim Yusuf Islam commented that the problem with the Muslim Manifesto was that the 'aspect of unity, idealistic as it may be, was not stressed except perhaps from a unilateral position'.[9] This comment reinforces the arguements put forward in this study that the Muslim community has not as yet constituted itself into an *Ummah* and that petro-dollar leadership can hardly convince the Muslim community of its credibility.

It is not possible for a community to live in isolation in a society when it is economically and politically dependent upon the British society and the British political system in the way that the Muslim community is. How, for example, can the Muslim community, in isolation, get any law through Parliament without a single Muslim or non-Muslim MP, even though its own 'Muslim parliament' may have passed resolutions? It is not by contravening laws but changing laws which are unjust that the Muslim community will significantly impact with British society.

The integrationist perspective is based on the assumption that British society is developing along multicultural lines because of different ethnic groups which have arrived in the country and have settled for a number of years. The integrationists believe neither in isolation nor in assimilation. On the contrary, they argue that respect for different cultures and religions should be cultivated. The above assumption is based on another assumption. It recognizes the fact that nobody migrated to Britain to change their culture and religion. They could have become secularized in their own countries of origin. The reality which prevails is that all migration tends to be for economic betterment. In relative terms, whatever the economic status of the migrants in their countries of origin, they have certainly improved that status in Britain. The class stratification among Muslims has been described in Chapter 2. In economic terms, therefore, every Muslim has integrated into the British economic structure.

In political terms, integration is weak. Although the Muslim community uses its power to vote for various politicians and parties, its power is still weak. It is weak because there is a lack of strength in united Muslim voting power.

In general, then, the scenario which emerges shows that the Muslims have integrated more economically than politically. They also lack a driving force and a source of inspiration. All three persepctives have limitations which force the development of the revolutionary perspective. It is based on the following assumptions.

Firstly, the revolutionary perspective starts with the assumption that Western culture is basically anti-Islamic. This hostility is not due to some personal reasons by heads of states, but is a course determined by Western history.[10]

Secondly, the revolutionary perspective is also based on the assumption that the Muslim community has not realistically made an assessment of its strengths and weaknesses in Britain. Its leaders are in the habit of talking big and reflect the truth of saying that 'empty drums make the most sound'. This situation has to be evaluated and the rhetoric and fantasy separated from reality and facts. Such evaluations can be derived only by arriving at the right conclusions or a realistic perception of reality.

Thirdly, the revolutionary perspective is based on the assumption that Muslims have to discard their reactionary Islam which is prevalent among Muslim communities in the West. Reactionary Islam arises as a response to the anti-Islamic tradition and hostility. Instead Muslims have to follow the *Sunnah* of the Prophet Muhammad. He was also confronted by a hostile anti-Islamic context when he started preaching about Islam. Yet he did not become a reactionary but a revolutionary.

Fourthly, the revolutionary perspective is based on the assumption that, without influencing or changing political realities, there can be no salvation for the Muslims. Just by having a Muslim name one does not become a Muslim. The Muslim community has to justify their migration Islamically. The Prophet and his Companions who went and settled in Madina were not sitting inactive. Along with the Muslims of Madina they actively worked and developed a strong Ummah whose political, social and economic dimensions were given serious attention. Furthermore, the Prophet and his companions did not rest content with their Hijra until they had converted Makkah to Islam, thereby establishing the first Islamic state.

In focusing on the Muslim community in Britain, they have all come as economic migrants with few, if any, exceptions. But Muslims can justify their stay in the West only if they can work for Islam. It is the opinion of a well-known scholar that 'I declare unequivocally that if your life and your stay here are beneficial to Islam your migration is not only justifiable but also an act of worship. I shudder at the thought...should we tell God that we came here only to earn our livelihood? Such a motive is not in the Islamic character; it does not befit a Muslim if you have taken due care that your faith remains unblemished, and you are associated with some Islamic endeavour...'[11] Islam is not a rigid religion as it has been made out to be. Every Muslim can justify his *Hijra* through making a conscious commitment to Islam. This commitment then has to come from within and has to be action-oriented by engaging in the welfare of the Muslim community and the Muslim world. It is not for personal but collective benefit.

Every Muslim must struggle against the four structures.

Every Muslim must struggle against the four structures. The forces supporting the racial, secular, internal colonial and the anti-Islamic are all becoming united against Islam. The struggle against these structures can only be fought on a political level, whether local or national. The Muslim community therefore has to actively engage or plunge itself into political participation within the British political system.

If Muslims really follow the *Sunnah* of the Prophet, then they have to follow his example. His *Hijra* to Madinah was not complete until he had established the Islamic state of Makkah. Muslims therefore have to help the genuine Islamic groups committed to transform the secular Muslim states (their countries of origin) into Islamic ones. But they have to distinguish the number of pseudo-Islamic groups in Muslim countries from the genuine ones. For example, in the case of Pakistan the Jamaat-e-Islami political party is considered to be a fundamentalist group. But this is far from truth, for the reality has been correctly depicted by a scholar who observes that 'on the one hand the leadership of tha Jamaat in the 1970s and 80s passed into non-ideological hands and it became extremely thuggish with university branches becoming gun-toting fascist paramilitary organizations. On the other hand, under Zia, the leadership became part of the circle of government and Jamaat enjoyed considerable government patronage and moved from religious radicalism to become an arch-conservative religious legitimiser of a military dictatorship. The Jamaat is represented in Britain by the Islamic Foundation in Leicester and the UK Islamic Mission. It...has negligible working class community links...but with Saudi money and support...its two organizations are avowedly propagandistic...but within the constraints of Saudi political and international interests'.[12]

Muslims in Britain have to understand why they must follow the *Sunnah* of the Prophet in order to convert their countries of origin into Islamic states. Had those countries been Islamic, colonialism would not have crept into Muslim lands, exploited them and left the countries so underdeveloped that the native Muslims had to leave for the West to search for economic livelihoods.

If Islam does not become the third force in the world to be reckoned with, the future of Muslims in Britain and for that matter anywhere else is at stake. Muslims therefore have to help all those Muslim groups engaged in the struggle in their countries of origin in order to make such states Islamic. This is the obligation of Muslims in Britain and elsewhere in Europe to the Muslim world.

Such help can take many forms and this study does not need to be specific as it falls outside its remit. Sufficient to state here that each political struggle has its own peculiar needs relevant for its success. The commitment of every Muslim should be to help other Muslims in Britain and the oppressed Muslim masses in the Muslim world.

Finally, while fulfilling their Islamic obligations to help less fortunate Muslims abroad from the oppression of tyrants they also have to fulfil their obligations in Britain. They have to be model citizens of Britain. They have to make significant contributions in the sphere of activities they are engaged in. But as this study has suggested, more political participation is needed for inputs on broader issues affecting Britain rather than those only affecting the Muslim community in Britain.

References

Chapter 1.

1. G.D. Mitchell, *A Dictionary of Sociology*. Chicago: Aldine Publishers, 1968, p. 47.

2. See: M. Iqbal Chaudhry, *Pakistani Society: A Sociological Analysis*. Lahore: Noorsons Publishers, 1968, pp. 102–4.

3. Muhammad Anwar, *Pakistanis in Britain: A Sociological Study*. London: New Century Press, 1985, pp.62–3.

4. E. Blunt, *The Caste System of Northern India*. Delhi: S. Chand & Co., 1969, p. 10.

5. Patricia Jeffery, *Migrants and Refugees: Muslim and Christian Families in Bristol*. Cambridge: Cambridge University Press, 1976, p. 31.

6. Muhammad Anwar, op. cit., pp.67–8.

7. See: Akbar Ahmad, *Religion and Politics in Muslim Society*. Cambridge: Cambridge University Press, 1983.

8. Zaki Badawi, *'Britain's Loyal Muslims'*. The Sunday Telegraph, 26 August, 1990.

9. See: F. Khan, *Sociology of Pakistan*. Dhaka: Shirin Publications, 1966.

Chapeter 2

1. See: Ivan Reid, *Social Class Differences in Britain*. London: Open Books, 1977.

2. See: B. Landry, *The New Black Middle Classes*. Berkeley, CA: University of California, 1987.

3. See: *'Britain's Browns'*. The Economist, 28 October, 1989.

4. See: Alison Shaw, *A Pakistani Community in Britain*. Oxford: Basil Blackwell, 1988, Chapter 7.

5. Graham Turner, *'Macho World of the Devout Capitalists'*. Daily Mail, 7 February, 1989.

6. Ibid.

7. *'Faith, Hope and Poverty'*. The Times, 18 August, 1987.

8. *'Muslims in the West'*. Newsletter of the Islamic Cultural Centre, No. 59, London, 1989, p. 4.

Chapter 3.

1. G.D. Qureshi, *Prophet for Mankind*. Leicester: Muslim Community Studies Institute, 1989.

2. Francis Robinson, *Varieties of South Asian Islam*. Research Paper No. 8, Centre for Research in Ethnic Relations. University of Warwick, Coventry, 1988, p.9.

3. Ibid., p.6.

4. Ibid., p.6.

5. Ibid., p.16.

6. Ibid., p.15.

113

7. *News of Muslims in Europe*, No. 39. Birmingham: The Centre for the Study of Islam and Christian-Muslim Relations, 30 April, 1987, pp. 8–10.

8. Ibid.

9. Francis Robinson, op. cit.,p. 10.

10. A. Hussain, *Vibrant Islamic Thinkers*. Telegraph & Argus (Bradford), 14 August 1987.

11. Ibid.

12. Ibid.

13. Ibid.

14. Ibid.

15. A. Gulf, *Terror Suspects Expelled*. The Guardian, 2 February 1990.

16. Ibid.

17. Muhammad Benaboud, *Orientalism and the Arab Elite*. The Islamic Quarterly, Vol. XXV, No.1 (1982), p. 7.

18. D. MacDonald, *Aspects of Islam*. New York, 1911, pp. 12–13. Quoted in A. Hussain, *Orientalism: The Ideology of Orientalism*, in A. Hussain et. al. (ed.), *Orientalism, Islam and Islamists*. Vermont: Amana Press, 1984, pp. 5–21.

19. Montgomery Watt, *Mohammad at Medina*. Oxford: Clarendon Press, 1956, pp. 199, 219.

20. Donald Smith, *Religion and Political Development*. Boston: Little Brown & Co., 1980 p. 11.

Chapter 4

1. Saad Eddin Ibrahim, *The New Arab Social Order: A study of the social impact of oil wealth*. Boulder, Co: Westview Press, 1982, pp.7—8.

2. Ibid., p. 111.

3. Iqbal Wahhab, 'Britain's Muslims told to toe Saudi line'. *The Independent*, 16 September 1990.

4. Ibid.

5. Ibid.

Chapter 5

1. Variables used by J.Booth, *'Political participation in Latin America'*. Latin American Research Review, Vol. X1V, No.3 (1979), pp. 30—61.

2. J. Nielsen, *A Survey of Local Authority Response to Muslim Needs*. Research Papers on Muslims in Europe, No 30/31. Birmingham: The Centre for the Study of Islam and Christian-Muslim Relations, 1986.

3. Moeen Yaseen, 'The Muslim View of Self-Determination. *The Times, Scottish Education Supplement*, 2 June 1989.

4. See: *The Islamic Banner (Manchester)*, February 1990.

5. Islamic Party letter dated 27 July 1989.

6. *New Life*, 15 September 1989.

7. Ibid.

8. *Financial Times*, 26 September 1989.

9. Marian Fitzgerald, *Political Parties and Black People*. London: Runnymede Trust Publications, 1984, p. 118.

10. Ibid., p. 104.

11. M. Anwar, *Pakistanis in Britain: A sociological study.* London: New Century Publishers, 1988, p. 140.

12. Michel Le Lohe, 'Problems of managing the Muslim vote'. *Muslim News,* 19 January 1990, p. 5.

13. Ibid.

14. See: *What Muslims can do.* London: The Muslim Educational Trust, 1988.

15. Michael Durham, 'The Religious Issue that won't go away'. *The Guardian* 14 March 1989.

16. J.M. Halstead, *The Case for Muslim Voluntary-Aided Schools.* Cambridge: The Islamic Academy, 1986, pp 67–68.

17. 'MacGregor firm on race decision'. *The Guardian,* 24 April 1990.

Chapter 6

1. See: *Newsletter of the Islamic Cultural Centre,* No. 39, April 1988.

2. D. Joly, *Making a Place for Islam in British Society: Muslims in Birmingham. Research Paper in Ethnic Relations No. 4, Centre for Research in Ethnic Relations. Coventry: University of Warwick, 1987, pp.6—7.*

3. *Nadeem Ahmad, 'Some reflections on the mosques in Britain'. Leicester, MCSI.*

4. *Amit Roy, 'House of Prayer stays faithful to its name'. Sunday Telegraph. 12 August 1990.*

5. *S.W. Barton, The Bengali Muslims of Bradford.* Leeds: Department of Theology and Religious Studies, 1986, p. 89.

6. Nadeem Ahmad, op. cit.

7. Moeen Yaseen, 'Role of Mosques in Pluralistic Societies'. Paper sent to MCSI. October 1990.

8. Nadeem Ahmad, op. cit.

9. Khalid Alavi, *Role of the Mosque in the Muslim Community.* Birmingham: Birmingham Central Mosque, 1989, p. 6.

Chapter 7

1. B. Jowell et. al., *British Social Attitudes.* Aldershot: Gower Publishing Co., 1989, p. 8.

2. Yusuf Islam, 'Voluntary Aided Muslims Schools'. Paper presented at a Muslim Education Forum held in Birmingham, January 1990, p. 7.

3. Ibid.

4. David Ward, 'Girls Want in from The Cold', *The Guardian,* 31 January 1989.

5. *The Sunday Times,* 10 August 1989.

6. Report by H.M. Inspectors on Muslims Girls High School, Bradford. Middlesex: Department of Education & Science, October 1986, p. 8.

7. S. Izruna, 'Improving Islamic Education in the Madrassah Schools the United Kingdom'. Report submitted to MCSI, Leicester.

8. Ibid.

9. Akram Khan Cheema, 'Education and the Muslim. Paper presented at the Council of Mosques Conference held in Bradford, 29 April 1990.

10. Fazlun Khalid, 'Progress and Pitfalls: Background to the Education of Muslims'. paper presented at the Muslim Education Forum, January 1990.
11. Zaki Badawi, 'Ingrained Racism brings Muslim Youth Back to Islam'. *New Horizon* (London), April-May 1988.
12. Mazher Mahood, 'Alarm over Mullahs who beat their Pupils'. *The Sunday Times,* 10 August 1986.
13. Afzalur Rahman, 'Islamic Education of Muslim Children in the West and the Problem of Curriculum and Syllabus', in M. Afendi and N. Baloch (eds.), *Curriculum and Teacher Education.*
14. S.A. Ashraf, *New Horizons in Muslim Education.* London: Hodder & Stoughton, 1985, p. 50.

Chapter 8

1. Ahmad Shafaat, 'Honest to God: A letter to Muslims in Britain'. Unpublished paper circulated by the author in 1981, p. 4.
2. Ibid.
3. See: 'Islam in Britain: At the crossroads of beliefs'. *The Times,* 17 August 1987.

Chapter 9

1. A. Hussain, *Muslim Youth and Westernization.* Leicester: Muslim Community Studies Institute, 1988, p. 11.
2. See: Graham Turner, 'Caught in the Culture Crossfire'. *Daily Mail,* 9 February 1989, p. 28.
3. Salim al-Hassani, 'The Muslim Youth of Britain'. Paper presented at the Muslim Education Forum meeting held in Birmingham, 20 January 1990.
4. Survey data from Muslim Community Studies Institute.
5. Dr Zaki Badawi, 'Ingrained Racism brings Muslim Youth back to Islam'. *New Horizon* (London), April-May, 1988, p. 25.
6. Salim al-Hassani, op. cit.
7. Ibid., p. 9.

Chapter 10

1. Survey data collected by the Muslim Community Studies Institute, 1989.
2. Survey communication with Muslim females (MCSI), 1990.
3. Kauser Mirza, *The Silent Cry: Second generation Bradford women speak.* Research Paper No. 43. Muslims in Europe Series. Birmingham: The Centre for the Study of Islam and Christian-Muslim Relations, 1989, p. 6.
4. 'Pakistani woman awarded £20,000 damages for slander over virginity'. *The Guardian,* 3 May 1990.
5. R. Sharif, *Interview with young Muslim women of Pakistani origin.* Research Paper No. 27. Muslims in Europe Series. Birmingham: The Centre for the Study of Islam and Christian-Muslim Relations, 1985, p. 4.
6. Kauser Mirza, op. cit., p. 11.
7. See: 'Muslim gets Life for Killing'. *Evening Mail,* 5 July 1989.
8. A. Roy, 'Why this girl wants a white husband'. *The Sunday Times,* 6 December 1987.

116

9. Michael Brake, *Comparative Youth Culture: The Sociology of Youth Cultures and Youth Sub-cultures in America, Britain and Canada*. London: Routledge and Kegan Paul, 1985, p. 141.

10. *Usra* (Milton Keynes), November 1989, p. 2.

11. Khalida Khan, 'Muslim women in Britain'. The Message (London), November-December 1989, p. 3.

12. G. Turner, 'Passion and the Models of Propriety'. *Daily Mail,* 8 February 1989, p. 27.

13. Ibid.

14. Survey Communication by MCSI, 1990.

15. Survey Communication by MCSI, 1990.

16. Survey Communication by MCSI, 1990.

17. Survey Communication by MCSI, 1990.

18. *The Guardian,* 31 January 1990.

19. Madeleine Bunting, 'A Meeting of Two Worlds'. *The Guardian,* 3 June 1990, p.21.

20. Ibid.

21. Farida Hussain (ed.), *Muslim Women.* London: Croom Helm, 1984, pp. 5-6.

Chapter 11

1. See: A. A. Izetbegovic, *Islam between East and West.* Indiana: American Trust Publications, 1984.

2. See: P. Clark, *Marmaduke Pickthall, British Muslim.* London: Quartet Books, 1986.

3. See: Abdel W. El-Affendi, *A false dawn. Inquiry* (London), January 1988, pp. 50-6.

4. Harfiyah Ball-Haleem, *Islamic Life: Why British Women Embrace Islam.* Leicester: Muslim Youth Education Council, 1987.

5. Survey Communication by MCSI.

6. Survey Communication by MCSI.

7. See: T. Williams (ed.), *British Women: Studies in Islamic Religious Experiences.* Leicester: Volcano Books (forthcoming).

8. See: *'British Converts Caught Between Two Cultures' The Independent,* 6 January 1990.

9. Survey Communication by MCSI.

10. Survey Communications by MCSI.

Conclusion

1. See: S. Qureshi, & J Khan, *The Politics of Satanic Verses.* Leicester: Muslim Community Studies Institute 1990.

2. P. Wintour, 'MP in furore over Muslims go home'. *The Guardian,* 29 August 1989.

3. Quoted in A. Maddison, *Class Structure and Economic Growth: India and Pakistan since the Moghuls.* New York: W.W. Norton, 1971, p. 4.

4. See: Speech delivered by the former Home Secretary, Douglas Hurd. at the Birmingham Central Mosque, 24 February, 1989.

117

5. See: The excellent paper by Akbar S. Ahmed, *Macaulay's Chickens: Asian Immigrants in Britain.* Sent to the Muslim Community Studies Institute.

6. *The Muslim Manifesto.* London: The Muslim Institute, 13 June 1990.

7. A. Jabeer, 'Institute Moves to Galvanise Popular Local Support'. *The Muslim News,* No. 16, 30 June 1990, p. 1.

8. See: Editorial, *The Muslim News,* No. 16, 30 June 1990, p. 2.

9. See: article: 'Shura as the road to unity' by Yusuf Islam, *The Muslim News,* No. 8, 31 August 1990. Also see the excellent book by Shabbir Akhtar, *Be Careful with Muhammad.* London: Bellew Publishing, 1989.

10. See: C. Tyerman, *England and the Crusades.* Chicago: Chicago University Press, 1988.

11. Syed Abul Hasan Ali Nadwi, 'Main Duty of Muslim Immigrants'. *Al-Nahdah* (Malaysia), Regional Dawah Council of South East Asia and the Pacific, 1984, p. 12.

12. See: the excellent paper by Tariq Modood, 'British Asian Muslims and the Rushdie Affair'. *Political Quarterley,* Vol. 61. No 2. April 1990 p. 152.

118

INDEX